Building Behavior

Building Behavior

The Educator's Guide to Evidence-Based Initiatives

Jessica Djabrayan Hannigan
and
John E. Hannigan

FOR INFORMATION:

Corwin

A SAGE Company

2455 Teller Road

Thousand Oaks, California 91320

(800) 233-9936

www.corwin.com

SAGE Publications Ltd.

1 Oliver's Yard

55 City Road

London EC1Y 1SP

United Kingdom

SAGE Publications India Pvt. Ltd.

B 1/I 1 Mohan Cooperative Industrial Area

Mathura Road, New Delhi 110 044

India

SAGE Publications Asia-Pacific Pte. Ltd.

18 Cross Street #10-10/11/12

China Square Central

Singapore 048423

Program Director: Jessica Allan

Content Development Editor: Lucas Schleicher

Senior Editorial Assistant: Mia Rodriguez

Production Editor: Tori Mirsadjadi

Copy Editor: Amy Marks

Typesetter: C&M Digitals (P) Ltd.

Proofreader: Sally Jaskold

Indexer: Maria Sosnowski

Cover Designer: Anupama Krishnan

Marketing Manager: Margaret O'Connor

Printed in the United States of America

Library of Congress Cataloging-in-Publication Data

Names: Djabrayan Hannigan, Jessica, author. | Hannigan, John E., author.

Title: Building behavior: the educator's guide to evidence-based initiatives / Jessica Djabrayan Hannigan and John E. Hannigan.

Description: Thousand Oaks, California: Corwin, 2019. | Includes bibliographical references and index.

Identifiers: LCCN 2019006518 | ISBN 9781544340081 (pbk. : alk. paper)

Subjects: LCSH: Behavior modification—United States. | School discipline—United States. | Restorative justice—United States. | Culturally relevant pedagogy—United States. | Affective education—United States.

Classification: LCC LB1060.2 .D52 2019 | DDC 371.39/3—dc23

LC record available at https://lccn.loc.gov/2019006518

This book is printed on acid-free paper.

Certified Chain of Custody

Promoting Sustainable Forestry

www.sfiprogram.org

SFI-01268

SFI label applies to text stock

19 20 21 22 23 10 9 8 7 6 5 4 3 2 1

CONTENTS

PBIS

Character Education

Restorative Justice

Culturally Responsive Teaching

Trauma-Informed Practices

SEL

Visit the companion website at
http://resources.corwin.com/BuildingBehavior
for downloadable resources.

ACKNOWLEDGMENTS

We wish to thank all the educators, researchers, practitioners, experts, and organizations for their contributions to the inspiration and knowledge in creating this book. To our immediate family, we could have not completed this book without your endless love, support, and babysitting services. Thank you to our loving children Riley, Rowan, and Baby John for being our biggest supporters. Our appreciation goes to the team at Corwin for recognizing this is a comprehensive guide for educators worldwide. Thank you for giving us the platform to share evidence-based behavior initiatives. To all who read this book, we thank you for doing what is best for students.

PUBLISHER'S ACKNOWLEDGMENTS

Corwin gratefully acknowledges the contributions of the following reviewers:

Ray Boyd
Principal
West Beechboro Independent Primary School
Beechboro, Western Australia

Faith Chaney-Grant
8th Grade English Language Arts Teacher
Springfield Public Schools
Springfield, MO

Shannon Hobbs-Beckley
Associate Principal
Graded American School of São Paulo
São Paulo, SP

Marcia LeCompte
Retired Elementary Teacher
Baton Rouge, LA

Vicki McFarland
Director of Federal Programs/Curriculum
Learning Matters Educational Group
Glendale, AZ

LaQuita Outlaw, EdD
Principal
Bay Shore Middle School
Bay Shore, NY

Mandy White
Science Teacher
Vicenza Middle School
APO, AE, Italy

ABOUT THE AUTHORS

Dr. Jessica Djabrayan Hannigan is an assistant professor in the Educational Leadership Department at California State University, Fresno. She works with schools and districts throughout the nation on designing and implementing effective behavior systems. Her expertise includes response to intervention (RTI) behavior, multi-tiered systems of support (MTSS), positive behavior interventions and supports (PBIS), social and emotional learning (SEL), and more. The combination of her special education and student support services background, school- and district-level administration, and higher education research experiences has allowed her to develop inclusive research-based best practices around systemic implementation of behavior initiatives throughout the nation. Some of her recognitions include being named California Outstanding School Psychologist of the Year, Administrator of the Year, Outstanding Faculty Publications and Service Award recipient, being recognized by the California Legislature Assembly for her work in social justice and equity, and the inaugural Association of California School Administrators Exemplary Woman in Education Award in 2017 for her relentless work around equity in schools.

Dr. John E. Hannigan is an executive leadership coach for Fresno County Superintendent of Schools in California. He has served in education for over 16 years as a principal, assistant principal, instructional coach, and teacher. Under his leadership, his school has received numerous awards and recognitions, including California State Distinguished School, Gold Ribbon School, Title I Academic School, Positive Behavioral Interventions and Supports (Platinum Level), and an exemplary RTI school for both academics and behavior. His school was selected as a knowledge development site for the statewide scaling up of multi-tiered systems of support (MTSS).

BUILDING BEHAVIOR
(The *Why*)

1

BUILDING EFFECTIVE BEHAVIOR INITIATIVES IN SCHOOLS

IN THIS CHAPTER you will find out why this book is needed, how it is designed to be used, and how to navigate through the behavior initiatives using the Behavior Initiatives K-W-L strategy for your school.

Section 1: The *Why* Behind This Book

Section 2: How to Use This Book: Building Behavior

Section 3: Behavior Initiatives K-W-L Strategy

SECTION 1: THE *WHY* BEHIND THIS BOOK

Schools and districts nationwide are experiencing a rapid increase in the number of students needing social/emotional and behavioral support to access their education. These increasing numbers have left some teachers, administrators, and parents at a loss. Now, more than ever, educators need to adjust, learn, and grow to meet the needs of the "whole" student. Students deserve to have access to school environments that are safe, welcoming, protective, preventive, tolerant, diverse, and supportive, and that have high expectations conducive to their academic learning as well as their social/emotional and behavioral needs. Creating school environments that meet these complex and sometimes invisible needs is challenging but worth the school's and district's investment of time and resources. To that end, educators need to implement behavior initiatives consistently and with a faithfulness to the cause they seek to correct.

Some compelling reasons for the *why* in this investment include the importance of building independence, resilience, self-regulation, problem-solving skills, and overall positive mental health for students, instead of using the traditional, exclusionary/reactionary practices. How students' social/emotional and behavioral needs are addressed in school is inextricably connected to their academic and social success; therefore, it is critical that implementation of behavior initiatives is made a top priority and is based on the needs of the students served. Furthermore, a strong positive correlation exists between behavior problems and low academic achievement (Gest & Gest, 2005; Cook, Landrum, Tankersley, & Kauffman, 2003). There is also a reciprocal effect by which behavior problems disrupt academic engagement. As a result, students may fail to master skills due to lack of engagement; by contrast, students in a highly engaged class with higher levels of academic achievement demonstrate fewer behavior difficulties (Payne, Marks, & Bogan, 2007).

Based on more than 20 years of research on discipline approaches, researchers have found that out-of-school suspensions and zero-tolerance approaches do not reduce or prevent misbehavior and are correlated with lower achievement (Irvin, Tobin, Sprague, Sugai, & Vincent, 2004; Losen, 2011; Mayer, 1995; Skiba & Peterson, 1999; Skiba & Rausch, 2006). Students who were suspended or expelled were more likely to be held back a grade or drop out of school, more so if they were disciplined repeatedly (Balfanz & Boccanfuso, 2007). In relation to this finding, 37 percent of students aged 14 and older with a mental health condition drop out of school; this is the highest dropout rate of any disability group (National Alliance on Mental Illness, n.d.).

Furthermore, children from all races and socioeconomic backgrounds experience and are impacted by trauma, which may manifest itself in students in social/emotional or behavioral forms. In fact, research suggests that between half and two-thirds of all school-aged children experience trauma that may affect their learning (Copeland et al., 2007; Felitti et al., 1998). According to the National Alliance on Mental Illness (n.d.), one out of five children aged 13–18 have or will have a serious mental illness (11 percent have a mood disorder, 10 percent have a behavior or conduct disorder, 8 percent have an anxiety disorder). Anxiety disorders are the most common mental health concern in the United States. An estimated 40 million adults in the United States (18 percent) have an anxiety disorder. Meanwhile, approximately 8 percent of children and teenagers experience an anxiety disorder. Most people develop symptoms before age 21. According to the Centers for Disease Control and Prevention (CDC), an estimated 9 percent of children aged 3–17 have attention-deficit/hyperactivity disorder (ADHD). Suicide is the third leading cause of death in youth aged 10–24 years, with 90 percent of those who died by suicide having an underlying mental illness. Seventy percent of youth in juvenile justice systems have at least one mental health condition, and at least 20 percent live with a serious mental illness (Skowyra & Cocozza, 2007).

As illustrated by these alarming statistics, students clearly have a variety of social/emotional and behavioral needs when they walk into our classrooms each day. Establishing a school campus that is equipped to respond to this diverse range of student needs requires close attention, across the entire system, to the identification and implementation of behavior initiatives for the long-term benefit of students as well as the adults serving them. Most educators would agree that this type of school environment is best for all students. However, the understanding of the *why*, *what*, and *how* of a specific behavior initiative selected for implementation and the process of continuous improvement are not always in alignment. As a result, many initiatives fail to be implemented successfully and are tossed aside in pursuit of the "next best thing."

The information in this book will help schools begin or refine the work of *building* behavior initiatives to meet the diverse needs of students rather than continuing to reach for the next best thing. Specifically, the book examines six common behavior initiatives.

SIX IDENTIFIED BEHAVIOR INITIATIVES

Positive Behavior Interventions and Supports

Character Education

Restorative Justice

Culturally Responsive Teaching

Trauma-Informed Practices

Social and Emotional Learning

Each behavior initiative is a research-based social/emotional or behavioral initiative designed to address the identified diverse needs of students. Before we discuss the information that will be provided for each of these behavior initiatives, we want to share some snapshots highlighting key characteristics of each. These identified behavior initiatives are *not in competition with one another but, rather, are inclusive in nature, based on the diverse needs of your students and depending on the intended outcomes for implementation.* Each of these initiatives is designed to serve a function or belief system around social/emotional or behavioral supports; therefore, it is essential that the selected initiative be implemented with fidelity.

Thoughts resonating with you so far:

_____

_____

_____

_____

_____

_____

_____

_____

Snapshots From Schools Implementing the Six Behavioral Initiatives

Positive Behavior Interventions and Supports (PBIS)

In a PBIS school, you may see three to five behavior expectations identified schoolwide, taught, posted, and reinforced in all settings of the school. Having a consistent language for behavior expectations and rules throughout all settings of the school is evident. You may see a tiered system of behavioral support interventions in place for students needing additional support. For example, there are procedures for collecting minor and major behavior data regularly in all settings, so the PBIS team has data to assign additional behavior reteaching opportunities for students. You may see "caught being good" tickets given to students demonstrating appropriate behaviors and possibly an incentive-type store (in person or online) set up for students to receive incentives in exchange for caught being good tickets or point systems. There may be clear and consistent routines and procedures in place for responding to discipline needs inside and outside of the classroom. You may also see positively stated signs posted throughout the school reinforcing the behavior expectations and rules of the school. Alternative forms of discipline are encouraged for students rather than the traditional exclusionary methods such as suspensions and expulsions.

Character Education

In a character education school, you may see monthly teaching and recognition around the identified character virtues. The teaching and reinforcing of these character virtues are more intrinsic in nature and connected to possible service learning opportunities schoolwide or by grade level or department. You may see banners posted with the character virtues throughout the school and hear them on all school announcements. You may see a character trait of the month identified, students and staff wearing a certain color for each character trait on specific days of the week, and student of the month awards given out around demonstration of these character traits. There is an ongoing focus on helping students to become positive members of the community.

Restorative Justice

In a restorative justice school, you may see classroom respect agreements created by the students in every class, classroom circles taking place weekly on student-selected or relevant topics, challenges, or needs of the students, school, or community. There is a focus on teaching all the educators and students the importance of coexisting in peace. You may see restoring relationship structures between student-teacher, student-student, and student-community. You may see youth court opportunities for students to help other students learn from their behaviors. Teachers work hard to establish relationships with their students.

Culturally Responsive Teaching (CRT)

In a CRT school, you may see teachers who can articulate and teach using a culturally responsive lens. Classrooms are managed with firm, consistent, loving control. Teachers are personally inviting, and the learning environment is physically and culturally inviting. Students are reinforced for academic development with high expectations. Teachers are the facilitators of a student-centered classroom environment. Students have a voice in their education; and their background, context, and culture are not only accepted and celebrated but also reinforced through the curriculum and instructional design to include culturally relevant references throughout all instruction. Instructional changes are made to accommodate differences in learners. CRT also provides a lens through which the teachers' and staff's perspectives on parents and the community are positive and united.

Trauma-Informed Practices (TIPs)

In a TIPs school, you may see teachers who understand the signs and symptoms of trauma and the effects it has on a child's brain development. Teachers are mindful that misbehavior is a reflection of a student's adverse childhood experiences (ACEs) and struggle to self-regulate. Teachers in a TIPs school don't view a child's behavior as "good" or "bad" but, rather, as "regulated" or "dysregulated." The six principles of a trauma-informed approach are embedded in the school system. For example, there may be opportunities in the classroom or in another room ("safe zone") for students to go to feel safe and calm themselves down when they get overwhelmed and need a break. You may see some play-based and other traditionally mental-health-based practices to support students in the school setting. Most important, the primary theme, or core value, of the school is modeled by every teacher: "You are safe here, we love you, and nothing is going to change that." When responding to challenging behaviors, teachers are sensitive to student experiences and invested in learning how to help struggling students by approaching misbehavior through the lens of "What happened to you?" rather than "What is wrong with you?"

Social and Emotional Learning (SEL)

In an SEL school, you may see the SEL core competencies taught and embedded into the curriculum or design in every classroom. For example, a school may have both direct teaching taking place in SEL with a curriculum, such as Second Step, as well as SEL instruction being integrated in reading, math, history, and other core subjects. Teachers are mindful of their own emotions and students' emotions. Teachers work hard every day to establish relationships with their students. Opportunities to understand and express emotions are provided for students. Professional development and training is provided to help students and teachers. You may see coordinated efforts throughout the school, classrooms, home, and the community. At an SEL school, diverse backgrounds and cultures are respected and ethical norms for behaviors are recognized by families, school, and community. Students understand the importance of having empathy for others and having a growth mindset in academic and social settings. Also, students are taught to set personal and academic goals and are supported in achieving them. In addition, at an SEL school, you will see alignment of schoolwide policies and practices and an environment with many family and community partnerships. Everyone is working as a team to help achieve school and community outcomes.

All too often we hear some of the following comments from educators, highlighting the need for this book:

"We don't really do PBIS anymore. We are more of a restorative justice school."

"We do not believe in buying behavior with incentives. We believe students should not be rewarded for doing what they are supposed to be doing, so we stopped implementing PBIS."

"We are grounded in the foundation of character education virtues. We do not believe in PBIS."

"We did not have enough resources to implement trauma-informed practices, so we are implementing culturally responsive teaching instead."

"We implement culturally responsive teaching districtwide because we had a racially fueled student situation at one of our schools that got to the board level."

"We don't call it PBIS or restorative justice. We call it social and emotional learning."

"We do not use the terminology of restorative justice in this district. We had teachers blame restorative justice practices for lax discipline policies in our schools."

"We tried PBIS and character education in our school, but it does not work for our students."

SECTION 2: HOW TO USE THIS BOOK: BUILDING BEHAVIOR

This book provides a guide for schools and districts to "build" behavior initiatives that are best suited for their school, based on the specific social/emotional and behavioral needs of the students they serve. It is designed to do the following:

- Help school staff understand the reasons behind implementing each of the behavior initiatives highlighted in this book and guide them in building effective behavior systems (i.e., selection, implementation, progress monitoring, and continuous improvement). *Note:* Even if a school is implementing one or a few of these behavior initiatives, staff should take the time to dig deeper into the identified best practices and resources or at least be willing to learn what other behavior initiatives can offer.

- Provide common definitions, frameworks, best-practice resources, and implementation tips; and identify the relationship of the key factors of each of the six behavior initiatives to John Hattie's Visible Learning work, which presents the world's largest collection of evidence-based research on the factors having the greatest impact on student learning (Hattie, 2018).

- Explain how to use what we call the SchoolWide Behavior Initiatives Process (SW-BIP) to select, self-assess, and build an application guide for effective implementation of one or a combination of the following behavior initiatives: positive behavior interventions and supports, character education, restorative justice, culturally responsive teaching, trauma-informed practices, and social and emotional learning.

We want to make building behavior initiatives in schools much less overwhelming by providing . . .

A general understanding of the purpose of each of the six behavior initiatives, rather than using their terms loosely or interchangeably

A practical resource that condenses the abundance of information available on each of the behavior initiatives

The knowledge needed to prevent the frequent replacement of one behavior initiative with another without assessing fidelity of implementation and effectiveness

Tools to examine which behavior initiatives are being implemented well and what can be added to or refined in existing implementation to improve outcomes for students

Best-practice resources presented in a practical way for each of the behavior initiatives

---

This book is *not* designed to replace a comprehensive training for any of these six initiatives, nor is it a substitute for any of the dozens of books written about them. Had that been the case, this book would have been the equivalent of a 1,500-page *Choose Your Own Adventure* book. What we have done is synthesize the comprehensive literature surrounding each behavior initiative; provide tools, links, and resources that are encompassed within each initiative; and take the work out of finding this information on your own. What you will see is well beyond anything you can just go out and Google.

Why didn't we provide a comprehensive summary of all approaches to each initiative? We included the commonalities of each initiative until we reached a saturation point and outlined the differences in order to give readers options for determining what they would prefer to explore more deeply. Obviously, any new approach to a specific initiative will come to fruition because a creator or author believes he or she has identified a gap in the way the initiative is written.

Summarizing them all under one description is impossible because of the subtle nuances each variation brings. Also, some purists feel strongly that their approach to the initiative is the only way and that anything different is in direct competition with theirs. We realize that some colleagues in the field will be critical of this book because it gives people options besides the one way of doing something that they have made a living training on. Our intention is to remain indifferent throughout: one approach is not better than another, and you, the reader, will have the ability to choose an option that is best for your site. We also take it a step further and give you the tools needed to see any initiative through to full implementation rather than scrapping it and moving on to the next one.

This book is designed to help educators understand the purpose for each of these six behavior initiatives and to provide a starting point with the best-practice resources available as schools or districts deciding to refine, add to, and/or build effective behavior systems. Essentially, this book is designed to be a "one-stop shop" to analyze the similarities and differences between each of the six initiatives and follow an initial SchoolWide Behavior Initiative Plan (SW-BIP) designed to help build the system.

As we began the difficult task of deciphering research, data, expert testimonials, and practical applications of the six behavior initiatives, common trends emerged. Specifically, similar reasons for implementation failure of each behavior initiative became visible, making it clear why this book is a necessary resource for educators.

Implementation Challenges and Tips for Avoiding Them

The work in this book allows you not only to understand the implementation challenges we see in schools and districts worldwide but also to learn how to build a higher level of behavior initiative implementation designed to prevent implementation failure. Fidelity of implementation is what students need. Before going through each of the six behavior initiatives in depth in the following chapters, it is important to understand some common implementation challenges and missteps we have personally witnessed and consider the tips provided to prevent them from impacting a successful implementation on your campus.

Thoughts resonating with you so far:

_____

_____

_____

_____

_____

_____

_____

_____

_____

Common Implementation Challenges and Missteps	Tips to Avoid Common Implementation Challenges and Missteps
Competing behavior initiatives: *lack of direction and purpose for each*	Make the implementation of behavior initiatives just as much of a priority as any academic initiative: *Make it clear that this is necessary for students to access their learning, and stay consistent with the message.*
A blend of components of behavior practices or initiatives (past and present): *lack of full implementation with fidelity*	Take the time to audit the implementation fidelity of behavior initiatives: *Understand the purpose of each initiative, set goals, and ensure best practices are being implemented.*
Moving from implementation of one selected behavior initiative to the next: *lack of consistency and clarity of outcomes; "the next best thing"*	Stay intentional and consistent with implementation rather than deviating from the implementation path as soon the first roadblock presents itself: *Progress monitoring and continuous improvement should be part of implementation; otherwise, a "this too shall pass" mentality will take over.*
Lack of understanding, training, building capacity around each behavior initiative	Make sure time is allotted for ongoing professional development and capacity building: *If proper ongoing professional development and capacity building is not a priority, then misconceptions around the behavior initiative will begin to blossom.*
Site and/or district administration beliefs and actions do not match	Leaders of the school *must* model what they preach: *If administrators do not believe in the reasons for implementation and continue using traditional approaches for behavior, then implementation will not work.*
A one-size-fits-all approach	Understand that the implementation of behavior initiatives is complex and requires equity (*fairness*) rather than equality (*sameness*): *Make clear that equity in implementation means giving individual students exactly what they need to access their education, not giving the same response to every student.*
Lack of a clear vision and expectations of the behavior initiative or structure to support implementation	Make the vision and expectations of implementation clear: *If staff decide to inconsistently implement bits and pieces of the initiative that they are comfortable with, rather than full implementation as designed, then it will not work.*
Lack of an accountability structure (i.e., progress monitoring of implementation effectiveness)	Ensure that a system exists to monitor whether implementation is truly taking place with fidelity throughout the school: *How accountability for implementation will be measured needs to be clear and consistent, and updated data need to be utilized with all stakeholders to make necessary adjustments in the implementation.*
Misconceptions around the behavior initiatives	Give staff ongoing opportunities to provide feedback and clarify misconceptions about implementation: *If misconceptions are not heard or addressed, they will plague implementation.*
Lack of behavior initiative alignment to district goals	Align behavior initiatives with at least one district-level goal around student wellness, or provide access to social/emotional supports similar to academics: *If not, implementation may not stay a priority.*
Lack of policy and district and/or school handbook alignment	Language in the policies and handbooks around discipline needs to support the core beliefs and implementation fidelity of the selected initiatives: *If the policies continue to reflect zero-tolerance practices or a black-and-white handbook approach to discipline, this does not coincide with the core beliefs of the six initiatives highlighted in this book.*
Lack of funding	Allocate funding not only for training but also for human resources to support implementation of these initiatives: *Language around implementation goals needs to be included in the funding formulas at the district and school site levels.*
Lack of expertise	Build the capacity of stakeholders and behavior specialists at the school and district around ongoing implementation needs: *Capacity building will help with implementation fidelity.*

We wanted to better understand the *why* around these common implementation missteps and challenges. As we dug deeper, it became clear that this is not a phenomenon that impacts only the implementation of behavior initiatives. We found that many improvement initiatives (academic or behavioral) begin as well-intended ideas and end up as just that—well-intended ideas. Some get off the ground briefly and are immediately labeled "full implementation." For example, schools worldwide have claimed to embrace the professional learning community (PLC) process, which is a research-based best practice. However, oftentimes the implementation is much less than what a desired full implementation should look like, which PLC founder Rick DuFour refers to as "PLC Lite." DuFour and Reeves (2016) note that too many schools have adopted the label without committing to the substance of the PLC process. They wrote that PLC Lite is an exercise in futility. This notion can be applied across any attempted initiative a school adopts without a full commitment to the substance of implementation, thus leading to a "Lite" version of that initiative.

For example, we have witnessed "PBIS Lite" as simply being the development and visibility of behavior expectations and rules in a schoolwide matrix (i.e., banners and posters), with rewards and recognitions, but those campuses refer to schoolwide PBIS being fully implemented. The most recent initiative for which we have seen this issue is Universal Design for Learning (UDL), a framework that acknowledges variability in the learning process. UDL principles include providing students with various ways to acquire, process, and integrate information and knowledge; options for navigating and demonstrating learning; and multiple means of engagement to tap individual learners' interests, challenge them appropriately, and motivate them to learn. Now, "UDL Lite" is spreading rampantly. A school may provide students with flexible seating and bouncy chairs and confidently declare, "We are implementing UDL."

We point this out to show how easily claims of full implementation and misconceptions based on partial implementation contribute to implementation challenges for any initiative. What's worse than an idea not getting off the ground? An idea getting off the ground incorrectly and being communicated to teachers and stakeholders as being implemented with fidelity, because now *it* gets the blame, instead of *its implementation* meriting the blame (as evidenced from some of the educator quotes listed after the snapshots presented earlier in the chapter).

Developing systems to respond to the social/emotional and behavioral needs of students must be approached the same way we develop a student's academic learning. Saying "we are just going to focus on PBIS this year" is akin to a school's staff declaring that they are "just going to focus on reading this year." Teaching only reading will lead to academic gaps in learning on a campus the same way a focus on only one aspect of a behavior system will lead to gaps in a learner's social/emotional development. An interdisciplinary unit being taught through language arts, science, and social studies is the academic equivalent of a school's staff looking through a trauma-informed lens while using PBIS practices to support students by teaching and reinforcing behavioral expectations across all locations of the school. In the same sense that English isn't competing against social studies, trauma-informed isn't competing against PBIS.

Our intent is for you to use this book as a guide to see how all six behavior initiatives work together and to clear up the misconception that some initiatives are in competition with each other. The intent is for you to have the tools needed to audit your system and identify *why* any of these initiatives are not working and to provide resources to get them functioning on your campus. Remember, it's not that *it* isn't working; it's the *implementation of it* that isn't working.

Consider the following questions about the current state of implementation of behavior initiatives at your school as you learn about the "chasm" of implementation outlined in the next section:

- To what extent can the school staff name the behavior initiatives being implemented at the school and the purpose for implementation for students?

- To what extent is training and ongoing professional development provided to the staff around the implementation of behavior initiatives at the school?

- To what extent are misconceptions about implementation of behavior initiatives impacting fidelity of implementation?

- To what extent is there alignment of implementation of behavior initiatives and school/district goals or intended student outcomes?

- To what extent do the adults at the school demonstrate the behaviors necessary for collective responsibility around implementation?

- To what extent do the adults at the school believe in the work?

- To what extent is the school getting the behavioral outcomes desired for students based on implementation?

- To what extent are the current challenges and roadblocks impacting fidelity of implementation?

Crossing the Chasm

For any initiative to get off the ground, there is a point where a "chasm" is reached that could stall the initiative and impede progress. Many initiatives fail to get off the ground because they cannot cross the chasm. Once this occurs, the "initiative" receives the blame as not being effective and the school or district moves on to the next best thing. Ultimately, it was the *implementation* that was not effective. Here we will describe the "Diffusion of Innovation" introduced by Everett Rodgers in 1962 and expanded by Geoffrey Moore in 1991 with "Crossing the Chasm." This model has been adapted and expanded many times since its inception. Diffusion of innovation is a theory that seeks to explain how, why, and at what rate new ideas expand or stall.

The innovation adoption lifecycle begins with the *innovators* making up 2.5 percent of your staff. These are the risk takers who have the resources and desire to try new things, even if they fail. Next are the *early adopters*, making up 13.5 percent of your staff. They are selective and considered to be "the ones to check in with" for new information; they reduce others' uncertainty about a new initiative by adopting it. Here is where the chasm begins (which we will explain shortly). Once the chasm is crossed, you've reached the "tipping point" or "critical mass." This group begins with the *early majority*, making up 34 percent of your staff. They will take their time before adopting a new idea. They are willing to embrace a new idea or initiative as long as they understand how it fits with their lives (job duties or role on campus). Next are the *late majority*, making up another 34 percent of your staff. They adopt in reaction to peer pressure, emerging norms, and/or necessity. Most uncertainty around an idea must be resolved before they adopt. Finally come the *laggards*, making up 16 percent. They are traditional and make decisions based on past experiences. They are unable to take risks on new ideas.

The point that will make or break the success of implementation is called the *chasm*. It's the point between the early-adopter stage and the early-majority stage. Figure 1.1 represents what crossing the chasm means by breaking into the mainstream, which is the most difficult and most important thing to get right. As the initiative is implemented and grows, those who haven't bought in yet will have high expectations and need convincing in order to get on board. The innovators and early adopters won't need huge reasons to jump on board with the initiative. But to get the early majority on board, that's exactly what you'll need. Early adopters see the need and the importance; they are buying the change and willing to move forward with this new initiative. They expect a clear discontinuity between the old and new. They will tolerate the glitches and bumps in the road during implementation. The early majority are buying this gradual development of improvement. However, they want to minimize the discontinuity with the old way. They will expect few glitches and a relatively smooth implementation.

If you're at the chasm right now, you may need to pivot your approach. Also, don't forget the laggards. They make up 16 percent of your staff and are your second largest adoption group. They are your skeptics and will resist change and need a slew of positive testimonials and first-hand accounts of success. Jim Knight (2018) states that if teachers are resisting, the first question that needs to be asked is, "Is there something I'm doing to engender this resistance?" There are two reasons staff will resist: (1) They don't think it's worth it, or (2) they don't think they can do it.

FIGURE 1.1 ■ Crossing the Chasm

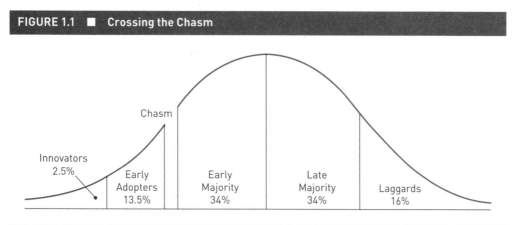

The chasm is the stalled implementation or growth of an initiative due to poor communication (or selling of the *why*) while you figure out how to sell to the early majority. As you can see, the first two segments are different from the others, and what works with them won't work for the others (see Figure 1.2). Early adopters may be newer teachers who hear the message and buy in to it; by contrast, the early majority are much more conservative with what they will endorse and support. They've seen initiatives come and go; they'll need convincing that this time it's different.

We will equip you with the tools needed to address the chasm by providing a comprehensive, practical, synthesized resource designed to guide decisions and demystify the misconceptions around implementation and provide clarity for decision makers using what we refer to in Part III as the SchoolWide Behavior Initiatives Process (SW-BIP). We provide a process to identify the problem through the SW-BIP, a causal system analysis to discover the root causes of the problem, a tool to separate and identify the individual barriers impeding implementation, and an action plan to initiate the process. In short, we will give you information on each of these behavior initiatives and a structure to help you assess and build successful implementation. We want to help you get past the implementation chasm and get these behavior initiatives rooted deeply into the culture of your school or district. Students are depending on it.

FIGURE 1.2 ■ Characteristics: Innovators to Laggards

Innovators	Early Adopters	Early Majority	Late Majority	Laggards
Visionaries and Enthusiasts		Mainstream Adopters		Resisters
• dream realizers • drive change • aren't afraid to fail • explore in iterations • high tolerance for risk, uncertainty, and ambiguity • adventurers • change initiators • internally motivated to change • respected by EAs; doubted by the mass	• evangelists • embrace change • self-efficacy • like to be first to try, use, engage, buy • try out new ideas in careful way • inspired by the new • like integrating new ideas in useful ways • influencers—like to convey ideas • respected by the majority	• pragmatists • accept change (sooner than LM) • deliberate • adopt if practical—weigh out pros and cons; think it out • go along; seldom lead • help it gain mass appeal • wait until it has been successful in practice	• skeptics • accept change (later than EM) • adopt after proven • often adopt out of necessity, not choice • go along w/peers • like to know rules creatures of habit • jump in when sees "everybody" is doing it	• change averse • value tradition • not leaders • suspicious of new innovations • often wait until forced to adopt • feel threatened or very uncomfortable by uncertainty and change • not going to buy in to new ideas

Source: Reproduced with permission from The Center for Creative Emergence, 2019. Original main sources: *Diffusion of Innovation* by Everett Rogers; *Crossing the Chasm* by Geoffrey Moore.

SECTION 3: BEHAVIOR INITIATIVES K-W-L STRATEGY

In each of the six chapters in Part II of this book (Chapters 2–7), you will find sections highlighted for each of the behavior initiatives based on information we synthesized from current peer-reviewed research findings, best practices in the field, practical application and experience, and expert input. The distinctive aspect of this book will be in the advice, the relationship to effect sizes, the best practices, and the putting it all together in Part III, where schools or districts apply this learning to practice using the SchoolWide Behavior Initiatives Process (SW-BIP). The SW-BIP will take you through the building, selection, self-assessment, and application guide development process of implementing behavior initiatives. For each of the six behavior initiatives, you will find

- The *what*

- The connection to Hattie's effect sizes in relation to the core components of the initiative

- Synthesized indicators of implementation success and challenges based on research findings

- A best-practice resource inventory (available electronically as well)

As you read through each chapter, reflect on the current practices in your school or district. Use the synthesized information from each chapter to help identify what you are attempting to achieve, implement, or refine in your school or district with regard to behavior initiative implementation. We understand this is an abundance of information. We encourage you to use the Behavior Initiatives K-W-L (Know, Want to Know, Learned) strategy as you read each behavior initiative chapter to take notes on what each behavior initiative is designed to accomplish and how it would apply to the students you serve (see Figure 1.3). The purpose of using this strategy as you read through Part II is to access background knowledge of the behavior initiatives and monitor your learning (synthesize the information, compare and contrast commonalities and differences, and, most important, understand the purpose and best-practice implementation of the behavior initiatives).

Thoughts resonating with you so far:

_____

_____

_____

_____

_____

_____

_____

FIGURE 1.3 ■ Behavior Initiatives K-W-L Strategy			
Behavior Initiative	**KNOW** (i.e., background knowledge, possible current implementation knowledge/state)	**WANT TO KNOW** (i.e., purpose, clarify misconceptions)	**LEARNED** (i.e., purpose, definitions, intended outcomes, effect sizes, critical components for implementation success, and best-practice resources)
Chapter 2: Positive Behavior Interventions and Supports			
Chapter 3: Character Education			
Chapter 4: Restorative Justice			
Chapter 5: Culturally Responsive Teaching			
Chapter 6: Trauma-Informed Practices			
Chapter 7: Social and Emotional Learning			

online resources ↘ Available for download at **http://resources.corwin.com/BuildingBehavior**

BEFORE YOU BEGIN: AN IMPORTANT NOTE

We understand that some behavior initiatives and/or programs are not highlighted in this book. We also understand that in different parts of the country (and world), some initiatives are emphasized more strongly than others. "Experts" in each of these fields are popping up who will disparage one initiative in favor of their own or who have a program to sell, thus promoting theirs as the only way and dismissing all others they feel are in direct competition. The behavior initiatives we have selected are based on our consistent findings through our research, application, and work with schools, districts, and county offices worldwide.

By the end of this book, you will not only have learned how to define and identify the critical components and best practices of each behavior initiative, but you will also confidently be able to decide which behavior initiative(s) best fit the needs of the students in your school or district. And you will have the information needed to build an effective system for implementation.

Our purpose in writing this book isn't to prove that one behavior initiative is better than another. Instead, we intend to lead the work of helping schools and districts adopt a process to identify their students' behavioral needs, select appropriate behavior initiatives focused on those needs, and build and implement best-practice behavior initiatives in a systemic and sustainable manner.

In Part II, you will find information on the following behavior initiatives: positive behavior interventions and supports (PBIS), character education, restorative justice, culturally responsive teaching (CRT), trauma-informed practices (TIPs), and social and emotional learning (SEL). Remember to use the Behavior Initiatives K-W-L strategy to help organize and document your learning as you read each chapter. Doing so will also equip you for Part III, where you will learn to use a tool called the SchoolWide Behavior Initiatives Plan (SW-BIP) to implement your learnings. This book is tabbed by section, giving readers the option to reference any chapter in Part II as a standalone section; however, it is recommended that you read all of them to get a comprehensive understanding before making decisions about implementation in your school or district. With that said, you will see the same description of effect sizes in Section 2 of each of the Part II chapters (on the connection to Hattie's effect sizes in relation to the core components of the initiative covered in the chapter). The redundancy is intentional; consequently, after reading this book, you can simply go back to any of the six chapters and access the same description of effect sizes rather than having to navigate back to the sole description as your only source of reference. We wanted to call this out beforehand so that you know the intentionality and logic behind it.

BUILDING BEHAVIOR
(The *What*)

PART TWO

POSITIVE BEHAVIOR INTERVENTIONS AND SUPPORTS

IN THIS CHAPTER you will find information on positive behavior interventions and supports (PBIS) divided into four sections, each followed by questions to consider to help you evaluate this behavior initiative and guide meaningful discussions around possible implementation in your school or district.

Section 1: The *What*—Positive Behavior Interventions and Supports (PBIS)

Section 2: Connection to Hattie's Effect Sizes in Relation to the Core Components of PBIS

Section 3: Synthesized Indicators of PBIS Implementation Success and Challenges

Section 4: PBIS Best-Practice Resource Inventory

SECTION 1: THE *WHAT*—POSITIVE BEHAVIOR INTERVENTIONS AND SUPPORTS (PBIS)

The goal of behavior support is not to create perfect children, but rather to create a perfect school setting for imperfect children (which is ALL children) to thrive and grow. Enter School A and you immediately notice warmth, support, joy, and excitement about learning from staff and all students. Enter School B and you notice tension, scolding, conflict, and frustration—from many staff and some students. Therein lies the spirit and science of positive behavior support, the goal of which is to use evidence-based processes and strategies to ensure that all schools are continuously striving to be the ideal exemplified in School A.

—Randy Sprick, PhD Safe & Civil Schools

Simply put, positive behavior interventions and supports (PBIS) is a structure for establishing a positive school climate by designing and providing behavior supports and interventions for all students' needs (Tier 1 schoolwide, Tier 2 targeted, and Tier 3 individualized) based on multiple data points. PBIS has a rich history in educational research and practice. However, there are some noteworthy variations in common PBIS definitions and styles of implementation. Even given the variations, the intended outcomes for PBIS implementation are similar.

Each chapter in Part II is divided into four sections that end with questions to help guide discussions with your teacher or leadership teams around each behavior initiative. As you navigate through this chapter, remember to use the Behavior Initiatives K-W-L strategy to help organize your learnings around PBIS implementation, beginning with the purpose for implementing PBIS and common definitions (i.e., the *what*).

Purpose for PBIS

- Create a positive school culture
- Use research-based strategies and interventions to help prevent and/or decrease problem behaviors
- Take a behavior-based systems approach to enhance the capacity of schools, families, and communities
- Focus on creating and sustaining Tier 1 (universal), Tier 2 (targeted), and Tier 3 (individual) systems of support
- Identify and teach behavior skills necessary for success in all settings
- Adjust the classroom or school environment to meet student needs

- Improve academics, attendance, and behavioral outcomes
- Address efficiency and equity of schools
- Improve school safety
- Address bullying
- Minimize exclusionary practices for discipline
- Improve social, emotional, and academic outcomes for all students, including students with disabilities and students from underrepresented groups

Variations of PBIS

Based on our experiences helping schools implement behavior initiatives and through our research findings, we have noticed that there are multiple definitions or variations of the six behavior initiatives outlined in this book. That can be overwhelming while you are trying to decide which behavior initiative is best for your school or district, so we outline three common definitions for each of the six behavior initiatives identified in this book, based on repeated mentions of them through the research and in the field. *Note:* If a definition you prefer is not cited in this section, it does not mean it is not a worthy definition to use. We just want to provide a few examples of common definitions to help educators better understand each behavior initiative. We strongly believe that school or district staff need to understand the *what* definition and the rest of the information in each of these chapters in order to make informed decisions about implementation.

THREE COMMON PBIS DEFINITIONS

Common Definition 1: Sugai and Horner (2010) define schoolwide PBIS as a systems approach to establishing the social culture and behavioral supports needed for all children in a school. PBIS is not a packaged curriculum but an approach that defines core elements that can be achieved through a variety of strategies. The core elements of PBIS are integrated within organizational systems in which teams, working with administrators and behavior specialists, provide the training, policy support, and organizational supports needed for initial implementation, active application, and sustained use of the core elements (Sugai & Horner, 2010):

Primary

- Behavioral expectations defined and taught
- Reward system for appropriate behavior
- Clearly defined consequences for problem behavior
- Differentiated instruction for behavior
- Continuous collection and use of data for decision-making
- Universal screening for behavior support

Secondary

- Progress monitoring for at-risk students
- System for increasing structure and predictability
- System for increasing contingent adult feedback
- System for linking academic and behavioral performance

- System for increasing home-school communication
- Collection and use of data for decision-making
- Basic-level function-based support

Tertiary

- Functional behavioral assessment
- Team-based comprehensive assessment
- Linking of academic and behavior supports
- Individualized intervention based on assessment information focusing on (1) prevention of problem contexts, (2) instruction on functionally equivalent skills and desired performance skills, (3) strategies for placing problem behavior on extinction, (4) strategies for enhancing contingence reward of desired behavior, and (5) use of negative or safety consequences if needed
- Collection and use of data for decision-making

Source: Reprinted with permission from PBIS.org, 2019. Text developed by Sugai, Horner, Lewis, 2015.

(Continued)

(Continued)

Common Definition 2: Sprick (2018) defines PBIS as "Safe & Civil Schools," an approach designed to help K–12 educators develop better behavior management strategies in schools, learn effective classroom management procedures, implement schoolwide positive behavior support and response-to-intervention for behavior, and design and implement a better school improvement plan. These processes include the following:

- *Using data.* Objective information about behavior is more reliable than labels, conclusions, or stereotypes.
- *Structuring for success.* All school settings should be organized to promote successful behavior from students.
- *Collaboration.* Helping students behave responsibly is the shared responsibility of all school staff.
- *Self-reflection.* If student behavior is irresponsible, school staff should reflect on what they can do to help students.

These processes and beliefs form a structure for procedures that help prevent students from falling through the cracks into school failure. The procedures can be categorized into three levels (Sprick, 2018):

- Schoolwide—affecting all students in all settings
- Classroom—for teachers in their own classroom
- Individual—specifically tailored to meet the needs of individual students

Common Definition 3: Hannigan and Hannigan (2016) define PBIS as the "PBIS Champion Model," which is a comprehensive systems approach for the design and delivery of PBIS in a school. This action-oriented framework provides *quality criteria* and *how-to steps* for developing, implementing, monitoring, and sustaining each level of the system: Bronze (Tier 1), Silver (Tier 2), and Gold (Tier 3). Each tier in the system consists of three categories: Category A—Markers, Category B—Characteristics, and Category C—Academic and Behavior Goals and the Work of the PBIS Team. Each category is composed of quality criteria and a set of defined actions (Hannigan & Hannigan, 2018a, 2018b; Hannigan & Hauser, 2015):

Tier 1 Markers

1. Establish and operate an effective PBIS team
2. Establish and maintain faculty/staff commitment
3. Establish and deploy effective procedures for dealing with discipline
4. Establish a data-entry procedure and design an analysis plan
5. Establish a set of schoolwide behavior expectations and rules
6. Establish a behavior reward/recognition program
7. Develop and deliver lesson plans for teaching schoolwide behavior expectations and rules
8. Develop and deploy a schoolwide PBIS implementation plan
9. Establish classroom systems—routines/procedures
10. Establish and execute an evaluation plan

Tier 2 Markers

1. Establish and operate an effective PBIS Tier 2 sub-team
2. Establish and maintain Tier 2 staff commitment
3. Establish a Tier 2 data-based process for identifying students
4. Establish a Tier 2 data-entry procedure and review plan
5. Establish a Tier 2 fidelity check process
6. Develop and deliver Tier 2 lesson plans
7. Establish a Tier 2 behavior incentive program
8. Establish a Tier 2 system for monitoring and communicating progress

Tier 3 Markers

1. Establish and operate an effective PBIS Tier 3 sub-team
2. Establish a culture and expectation for supporting all students
3. Conduct a Tier 3 resource inventory
4. Establish a Tier 3 timely response plan
5. Establish a Tier 3 fidelity check process

Source: Hannigan & Hauser, 2015; Hannigan & Hannigan, 2016; Hannigan & Hannigan, 2018.

In Chapter 1 of this book, we shared a snapshot of a PBIS school as a reference. We also want to provide a before-and-after story to help reinforce the beliefs and behaviors necessary for implementing PBIS in your school or district.

A BEFORE-AND-AFTER PBIS STORY

Before PBIS . . . it felt as if our school was out of control. Teachers felt overwhelmed with discipline. There were no processes for identifying students in need of additional behavioral support. Our responses were very reactive in nature and exhausting for all involved. It truly felt like the students were running the school. Teachers were very unhappy and did not want to come to school. Many were using their personal days to stay home rather than come to school. The teacher union was involved due to the number of teachers feeling burned out and contacting their union representation for support.

After PBIS . . . the school "just felt different" for everyone. The clear and consistent behavior expectations and rules along with the systemic procedures in place to respond to minor and major behaviors in and out of the classroom helped the school feel more preventive rather than always reactive and in crisis mode. The common language and procedures helped open the communication lines between the teachers and administrators and allowed for reteaching and individualized opportunities to be put into place in a timely fashion for students who needed additional supports or interventions to access their education. PBIS also helped provide a structure for helping teachers who needed additional supports with student behavior prior to them escalating to the next level.

Section 1: Questions to Consider

What are the intended outcomes of your school's or district's PBIS initiative?

_____

_____

_____

_____

_____

_____

_____

_____

_____

_____

(Continued)

(Continued)

How does your school or district define PBIS?

_____

_____

_____

_____

_____

_____

_____

_____

What is currently in place at your school or district?

_____

_____

_____

_____

_____

_____

_____

_____

What would your next steps be, given what you have read so far?

_____

_____

_____

_____

_____

_____

_____

_____

SECTION 2: CONNECTION TO HATTIE'S EFFECT SIZES IN RELATION TO THE CORE COMPONENTS OF PBIS

Why Hattie's Effect Sizes?

In looking at what information about PBIS would be helpful for educators, we went back to the question of what works best in education. That question also drove Hattie's comprehensive meta-analysis of areas that contribute to learning: the student, the home, the school, the classroom, the curricula, the teacher, and teaching and learning approaches (Hattie, 2018). Along with providing information on the relative effects of these influences on student achievement, Hattie also emphasized the importance of understanding and making visible the story of the underlying data. One of his most critical findings was how important it is to make teaching and learning visible. We agree and feel the same about making the teaching and learning of *behavior* visible. We've compared key components of PBIS to influences Hattie identifies that impact student achievement. We feel these components are intrinsically linked to supporting a student's social emotional needs, and provide further evidence of the *why*; that is, implementation of these behavior initiatives is also critical to supporting a student's academic achievement. The following definition of key terms and description of how to interpret effect sizes will be a useful reference as you review the PBIS table in this section.

HOW TO INTERPRET EFFECT SIZES

Hattie's work is based on achievement outcomes, while this book focuses on behaviors. We know that misbehavior can take away from students' achievement outcomes. A 1.0 standard deviation is typically associated with an increase in student achievement by two to three years. An effect size of 1.0 would mean that, on average, students receiving that treatment would exceed 84 percent of students not receiving the treatment. Hattie (2009) sets the benchmark of an effect size of $d = 0.4$ as the "hinge-point" where anything above it is labeled in the "zone of desired effects" as influences with the greatest impact on student learning. That doesn't mean that anything below 0.4 shouldn't be explored in greater detail. It just means that the influences aren't as great. Effects between $d = 0.15$ and $d = 0.40$ are typically what teachers could accomplish across an ordinary year of teaching. Ninety-five percent of everything we do has a positive influence on achievement, so setting the benchmark at anything above zero would be pointless. Furthermore, the zone between $d = 0.0$ and $d = 0.15$ is what students could achieve without schooling or by the simple process of maturation alone. Therefore, any effects below $d = 0.15$ are potentially harmful and should not be implemented. The remaining 5 percent of the factors have reverse effects, or decrease achievement. To put it simply, Hattie (2009) says that "students who do not achieve at least 0.40 improvement in a year are going backwards" (p. 250). Additionally, "It is a teacher who does not achieve an average of $d > 0.40$ per year that I do not want my children to experience" (p. 126).

Hattie presents his research through seven main contributors to learning (referred to as sources of influence): *the student, curricula, home, school, classroom, teacher, and teaching and learning approaches.* Hattie works through each of these sources of influence to evaluate which specific innovations and influences (factors) have the greatest impact on achievement. The factors are grouped by more specific "aspects" of each source of influence.

Visualize it like this:

1. **School (*source of influence*)**
   a. Other school factors (*aspect*)
      i. Suspension/expelling students (*factor*) (effect size [d] = –0.20)

2. **Classroom (*source of influence*)**
   a. Classroom influences (*aspect*)
      i. Decreasing disruptive behavior (*factor*) ($d = 0.34$)

The data in the table are listed from lowest effect size to highest. Remember, each source of influence is the broader category, and the subsets of each source are the aspects, which then group the various factors for each subset.

PBIS: Connection to Hattie's Effect Sizes in Relation to Core Components of This Behavior Initiative			
Source of Influence	**Aspect**	**Factor**	**Effect Size**
Student	Physical influences	ADHD	−0.9
School	Other school effects	Suspending or expelling students	−0.2
School	Leadership	School climate	0.32
Classroom	Classroom influences	Decreasing disruptive behavior	0.34
School	Other school effects	Counseling effects	0.35
Classroom	Classroom influences	Classroom management	0.35
Curricula	Play programs	Social skills programs	0.4
Classroom	Classroom influences	Classroom cohesion	0.44
Teaching: student learning strategies	Learning strategies	Time on task	0.49
Home	Family dynamics	Parental involvement	0.5
Teacher	Teacher-student interactions	Teacher-student relationships	0.52
Classroom	Classroom influences	Peer influences	0.53
School	Preschool experiences	Preschool with at-risk students	0.56
Classroom	Classroom influences	Classroom behavior	0.62
Teaching: teaching/instruction strategies	Strategies emphasizing feedback	Response to intervention	1.29

Source: Hattie, J. (2018, October). *Visible Learning^plus 250+ influences on student achievement.* Retrieved from https://us.corwin.com/sites/default/files/250_influences_10.1.2018.pdf. Retrieved February 4, 2019.

Educators tend to focus on the influences that have the most positive effects on student learning (those at the bottom of the preceding list), using that information to decide what to do more of. They don't generally look at the top of the list to identify what to do less of. Understanding this list from a strength and deficit lens allows educators to become more cognizant of the factors they influence directly, allowing them to target the effects these influences have on learning (e.g., by continuing, decreasing, or ending altogether certain practices) in order to create environments that reverse negative effects and increase positive effects on student success.

For example, suspensions and expulsions have a −0.2 effect size on student achievement, which equates to a negative (or reverse) effect on learning. Knowing the negative effect that suspensions have on student achievement, administrators can continue to use suspensions as a means of discipline or they can reserve the right to use suspensions only for the most egregious of offenses.

We encourage you to use this information to help guide implementation of behavior initiatives.

Section 2: Questions to Consider

What connections can you make between the effect sizes of the common components of implementation of PBIS and academic achievement?

_____

_____

_____

_____

_____

_____

_____

_____

_____

_____

How will you use effect sizes to ask questions that will allow you to dig deeper to improve practice?

_____

_____

_____

_____

_____

_____

_____

_____

_____

_____

_____

_____

(Continued)

(Continued)

How will you use this information with your colleagues to achieve the desired outcomes for students?

_____

_____

_____

_____

_____

_____

_____

_____

_____

_____

_____

_____

_____

_____

_____

_____

_____

_____

SECTION 3: SYNTHESIZED INDICATORS OF PBIS IMPLEMENTATION SUCCESS AND CHALLENGES

To develop this synthesized list of indicators of PBIS implementation success and challenges, we relied on our research and experiences as practitioners. Specifically, we used a combination of peer-reviewed research findings, practical application and experiences from the field, and expert testimonials as our reference to identify common implementation success trends and challenge trends. We wanted to provide this information as you consider implementation of this behavior initiative.

PBIS: Synthesized Indicators of Implementation Success and Challenges	
Implementation Success Trends	**Implementation Challenge Trends**
Administrator support and belief	Lack of administration support
Staff belief	Lack of staff collective agreement around implementation
High expectations	
Clarity around implementation	Misconceptions about implementation
Funding secured	Lack of clear communication and messaging
District guideline and policy alignment	Misconceptions that PBIS replaces discipline
Ongoing education and training provided	Lack of understanding that it is a tiered system
Ongoing input on implementation collected and utilized	Competing initiatives
	Not a school priority
Community and stakeholder buy-in	Led by only a handful and not by the majority of the school staff
Setting implementation SMART goals for each tier of supports	Misconception that PBIS is simply banners, tickets, and incentives
Training on each tier of implementation	
Clarity in roles and responsibilities for implementation	Not using data
Accountability measures in place	Principal delegates implementation responsibilities to others
Flexibility and innovation allowed for implementation	

Section 3: Question to Consider

To what extent will you use the synthesized indicators of implementation success and challenges to prevent obstacles during implementation?

_____

_____

_____

_____

_____

_____

_____

_____

_____

_____

_____

_____

_____

_____

_____

_____

_____

_____

_____

_____

_____

_____

SECTION 4: PBIS BEST-PRACTICE RESOURCE INVENTORY

To develop this best-practice resource inventory for PBIS implementation, we again used as our reference points a combination of research and best practices in the field based on our experiences. For example, we included effective resources based on (1) peer-reviewed research findings and (2) data from schools and districts implementing PBIS with effective outcomes for students. This information could be used as a starting point for looking into best-practice resources to assist with your implementation of PBIS. *Note:* We understand that other resources are available. What is provided here is what we found based on the aforementioned criteria for this best-practice resource inventory.

PBIS: Best-Practice Resource Inventory		
Resource	**Description** *Note:* **Some of the descriptions in this column are quoted directly from the listed resources.**	**References**
Florida Positive Behavioral Interventions & Support Project A Multi-Tiered System of Supports Website	This website is designed to provide training opportunities, resources, and technical assistance to districts in the development and implementation of positive behavioral interventions and supports at the school-wide (Tier 1), classroom, targeted group (Tier 2), and individual student (Tier 3) levels.	http://flpbis.cbcs.usf.edu/about/PBIS.html
Randy Sprick's Safe & Civil Schools: CHAMPS	The CHAMPS program is designed to put in place an effective behavior classroom management system. Specifically, designed to • Improve classroom behavior (on-task, work completion, cooperation), • Establish clear classroom behavior expectations with logical and fair responses to misbehavior, • Motivate students to put forth their best efforts (perseverance, pride in work), • Reduce misbehavior (disruptions, disrespect, non-compliance), • Increase academic engagement, resulting in improved test scores, • Spend less time disciplining students and more time teaching them, • Teach students to behave respectfully and to value diversity, thereby reducing cultural differences that may manifest as misbehavior, • Feel empowered and happy to be in the classroom, • Develop a common language about behaviors among all staff, • Create a plan for orienting and supporting new staff, and • Reduce staff burnout.	http://www.safeandcivilschools.com/products/scs_overview.php
PBIS Champion Model	The PBIS Champion Model is a practical PBIS framework designed based on best-practice implementation of PBIS/MTSS/RTI in each tier of support. This model provides a method of schools to audit, implement, and/or refine each tier of implementation.	pbischampionmodelsystem.com
PBISworld.com website	PBISworld.com is an online resource site for the broader PBIS community.	https://www.pbisworld.com/

(Continued)

PBIS: Best-Practice Resource Inventory (Continued)		
Resource	**Description** *Note:* **Some of the descriptions in this column are quoted directly from the listed resources.**	**References**
OSEP Technical Assistance Center on Positive Behavioral Interventions and Supports	The PBIS Network provides PBIS support, training, and resource opportunities for schools and districts implementing PBIS throughout the nation. This website provides the contact information for regional or state PBIS coordinators who provide technical support on PBIS implementation. The Technical Assistance Center on PBIS supports schools, districts, and states to build systems capacity for implementing a multi-tiered approach to social, emotional, and behavior support.	https://www.pbis.org/
Hands Off Academy	Hands Off Academy is a behavior intervention designed to intentionally teach students how to keep their hands to themselves.	pbischampionmodelsystem .com
Check & Connect	Check & Connect is an intervention used with K–12 students who show warning signs of disengagement with school and who are at risk of dropping out. At the core of Check & Connect is a trusting relationship between the student and a caring, trained mentor who both advocates for and challenges the student to keep education salient. Students are referred to Check & Connect when they show warning signs of disengaging from school, such as poor attendance, behavioral issues, and/or low grades.	http://www.checkand connect.umn.edu/model/ default.html
Responding to Problem Behavior in Schools: The Behavior Education Program, 2nd edition	This bestselling book has been used in schools across the country to establish efficient and cost-effective systems of Tier II positive behavior support. The Behavior Education Program (BEP) was developed for the approximately 10–15% of students who fail to meet schoolwide disciplinary expectations but do not yet require intensive, individualized services. Clear, step-by-step guidelines are provided for implementing the approach, which incorporates daily behavioral feedback, positive adult attention, and increased home–school collaboration.	Crone, Hawken, and Horner (2010)
Olweus Bully Prevention	The Olweus Program (pronounced Ol-VAY-us) is a comprehensive approach that includes schoolwide, classroom, individual, and community components. The program is focused on long-term change that creates a safe and positive school climate. It is designed and evaluated for use in elementary, middle, junior high and high schools (K–12). The program's goals are to reduce and prevent bullying problems among schoolchildren and to improve peer relations at school. The program has been found to reduce bullying among students, improve the social climate of classrooms, and reduce related antisocial behaviors, such as vandalism and truancy.	http://olweus.sites.clemson .edu/
Don't Suspend Me! An Alternative Discipline Toolkit	*Don't Suspend Me!* gives educators the tools they need to apply alternative discipline methods. Includes a toolkit with alternative strategies to use for the most common behavior challenges and worksheets and exercises for the major discipline incidents that occur in schools throughout the nation.	Hannigan and Hannigan (2017)
Leaps Website/ Behavior Lessons	Leaps operationalizes PBIS initiatives. It is the platform that provides content, assessments, progress, fidelity data, and training resources.	https://selforschools.com/ pbis/rti

PBIS: Best-Practice Resource Inventory		
Resource	**Description** *Note:* Some of the descriptions in this column are quoted directly from the listed resources.	**References**
First Step to Success	First Step to Success is an early intervention program designed to help children who are at risk for developing aggressive or antisocial behavioral patterns. The program uses a trained behavior coach who works with each student and his or her class peers, teacher, and parents for approximately 50 to 60 hours over a three-month period. First Step to Success includes three interconnected modules: screening, classroom intervention, and parent training. The screening module is used to identify candidates who meet eligibility criteria for program participation. Classroom intervention and parent training comprise the program intervention component of First Step to Success.	Epstein and Walker (2002)
The Tough Kid Series	The Tough Kid Series is a comprehensive library of practical, research-based strategies that help you deal with a range of behavioral issues.	http://www.toughkid.com/
Ripple Effects	Multi-tiered, digital system of personalized interventions and behavioral supports (MTSS)	https://rippleeffects.com/
Association for Positive Behavior Support (APBS)	The Association for Positive Behavior Support is an active body, focusing its attention on dissemination, education, and public policy efforts. It manages and links websites on PBS practices, systems and examples, engages in policy development around the provision of behavior support, works to establish national standards that define competency in the application of positive behavior support, encourages the training of professionals skilled in PBS practices through the development of training materials and the embedding of PBS content in relevant professional certificate and degree programs.	http://apbs.org/index.html
PBIS Rewards Website	PBIS Rewards is a Software-as-a-Service solution that provides an automated schoolwide PBIS management system. With PBIS Rewards, school administration can clearly see how teachers are utilizing PBIS and how PBIS is improving school culture.	https://www.pbisrewards.com/about/
Seven Steps for Developing a Proactive Schoolwide Discipline Plan: A Guide for Principals and Leadership Teams, 2nd edition	This book offers seven procedural steps to build a proactive schoolwide discipline plan that maximizes teaching and learning, prevents problem behaviors, and maintains desirable behavior to enhance school success. Get started in creating a positive and supportive environment by learning how to: • Develop, teach, and maintain school-wide behavior expectations • Correct problem behaviors • Sustain your plan for the long haul	Colvin and Sugai (2018)
The PBIS Tier One, Two, and Three Handbook series	This action-oriented PBIS framework series of handbooks provides *quality criteria* and *how-to steps* for developing, implementing, monitoring, and sustaining each level of the system: Bronze (Tier 1), Silver (Tier 2), and Gold (Tier 3). Each tier in the system consists of three categories: Category A—Markers, Category B—Characteristics, and Category C—Academic and Behavior Goals and the Work of the PBIS Team. Each category is composed of quality criteria and a set of defined actions.	Hannigan and Hauser (2015); Hannigan and Hannigan (2018a, 2018b)
Center for Behavior Education and Research (CBER)	The purpose of CBER is to conduct rigorous research and translate and disseminate empirically supported practices that promote equity and improve educational outcomes for all learners, especially those with or at risk for learning and behavioral difficulties.	https://cber.uconn.edu/?utm_source=cberorg&utm_medium=web&utm_campaign=redirect

Section 4: Questions to Consider

What resources do you think would help with your implementation of this behavior initiative?

_____

_____

_____

_____

_____

_____

_____

_____

_____

Name one resource listed that you will investigate further and why.

_____

_____

_____

_____

_____

_____

_____

_____

_____

_____

CHARACTER EDUCATION

IN THIS CHAPTER you will find information on character education divided into four sections, each followed by questions to consider to help you evaluate this behavior initiative and guide meaningful discussions around possible implementation in your school or district.

Section 1: The *What*—Character Education

Section 2: Connection to Hattie's Effect Sizes in Relation to the Core Components of Character Education

Section 3: Synthesized Indicators of Character Education Implementation Success and Challenges

Section 4: Character Education Best-Practice Resource Inventory

SECTION 1: THE *WHAT*— CHARACTER EDUCATION

A focus on character strengthens individuals and whole communities. When everyone is on the same page and working toward shared goals, they're more likely to be successful. While the character journey is never-ending, more intentionality in these areas leads to more thoughtful learning, stronger skill development, and better relationships.

—**Sheril Morgan** Director, Schools of Character

Simply put, character education is a structure for teaching and modeling essential character virtues that students need in order to become productive members of the community. However, there are some noteworthy variations in common character education definitions and styles of implementation. Even given the variations, the intended outcomes for character education implementation are similar.

Each chapter in Part II is divided into four sections that end with questions to help guide discussions with your teacher or leadership teams around each behavior initiative. As you navigate through this chapter, remember to use the Behavior Initiatives K-W-L strategy to help organize your learnings around character education implementation, beginning with the purpose for implementing character education and common definitions (i.e., the *what*).

Purpose for Character Education

- Create a positive school culture
- Promote prosocial competencies
- Improve school-based outcomes
- Increase general social-emotional functioning
- Improve socio-moral cognition
- Increase prosocial behaviors and attitudes
- Teach problem-solving skills
- Prevent drug use

- Prevent violence and aggression
- Improve school behavior
- Teach emotional competency
- Improve academic achievement
- Increase attachment to school
- Address general misbehavior
- Teach and model personal morality
- Develop character knowledge

Variations of Character Education

Based on our experiences helping schools implement behavior initiatives and through our research findings, we have noticed at times there are multiple definitions or variations of the six behavior initiatives outlined in this book. That can be overwhelming while you are trying to decide which behavior initiative is best for your school or district, so we outline three common definitions for each of the six behavior initiatives identified in the book, based on repeated mentions of them through the research and in the field. *Note:* If a definition you prefer is not cited in this section, it does not mean it is not a worthy definition to use. We just want to provide a few examples of common definitions to help educators better understand each behavior initiative.

We strongly believe that school or district staff need to understand the *what* definition and the rest of the information in each of these chapters in order to make informed decisions about implementation.

THREE COMMON CHARACTER EDUCATION DEFINITIONS

Common Definition 1: Character education is a national movement creating schools that foster ethical, responsible, and caring young people by modeling and teaching good character through emphasis on universal values that we all share. It is the intentional, proactive effort by schools, districts, and states to instill in their students important core, ethical values such as caring, honesty, fairness, responsibility, and respect for self and others. Character education is the deliberate effort to develop good character based on core virtues that are good for the individual and good for society. Based on prior work by Kevin Ryan and by Thomas Lickona, the Character Education Partnership has defined character into three broad categories:

1. Understanding (the "head"),

2. Caring about (the "heart"), and

3. Acting upon core ethical values (the "hand")

Common Definition 2: Character education, as defined in the "11 Principles of Effective Character Education," is based on guidelines developed by educators, researchers, and experts to develop students with strong character and a positive school culture (http://character.org/more-resources/11-principles/):

1. The school community promotes core ethical and performance values as the foundation of good character.

2. The school defines "character" comprehensively to include thinking, feeling, and doing.

3. The school uses a comprehensive, intentional, and proactive approach to character development.

4. The school creates a caring community.

5. The school provides students with opportunities for moral action.

6. The school offers a meaningful and challenging academic curriculum that respects all learners, develops their character, and helps them to succeed.

7. The school fosters students' self-motivation.

8. The school staff is an ethical learning community that shares responsibility for character education and adheres to the same core values that guide the students.

9. The school fosters shared leadership and long-range support of the character education initiative.

10. The school engages families and community members as partners in the character-building effort.

11. The school regularly assesses its culture and climate, the functioning of its staff as character educators, and the extent to which its students manifest good character.

Source: Reprinted with permission from Character.org, 2019.

Common Definition 3: "The intentional attempt in schools to foster the development of students' psychological characteristics that motivate and enable them to act in ethical, democratic, and socially effective and productive ways" (Berkowitz, Althof & Bier, 2012, p. 72). The framework is called the PRIMED model, an acronym for six principles of effective character education: Prioritization, Relationships, Intrinsic Motivation, Modeling, Empowerment, Developmental Pedagogy (Berkowitz, Bier, & McCualey, 2017, p. 38).

In Chapter 1 of this book, we shared a snapshot of a character education school as a reference. We also want to provide a before-and-after story to help reinforce the beliefs and behaviors necessary for implementing character education in your school or district.

A BEFORE-AND-AFTER CHARACTER EDUCATION STORY

Before character education . . . it felt like we were missing the opportunity to teach virtues and ethical values to our students. The majority of the veteran teachers felt like students were behaving only when provided extrinsic motivations, and they voiced their concerns about students doing the right thing in school and in the community even when no one was watching or providing them with a reward. Rewards and punishments were the premise of classroom and school discipline. Traditional classroom structures were in place where students did not have a voice in the rules, norms, and solutions.

After character education . . . it felt like everyone was on the same page around the need for teaching and modeling good character and behavior. The idea of a caring community was reinforced by all staff. Students were given the opportunity to learn about key values such as fairness, respect, honesty, and integrity through activities such as service learning opportunities designed to give back to the community. Having opportunities to problem solve and learn from mistakes was the premise of classroom and school discipline. A more democratic classroom structure was evident in all classrooms where students had a voice in the rules, norms, and solutions for classroom, schoolwide, and community solutions and problem solving.

Section 1: Questions to Consider

What are the intended outcomes of your school's or district's character education initiative?

_____

_____

_____

_____

_____

_____

_____

_____

How does your school or district define character education?

_____

_____

_____

_____

_____

_____

_____

_____

_____

What is currently in place at your school or district?

_____

_____

_____

_____

_____

_____

_____

_____

What would your next steps be, given what you have read so far?

_____

_____

_____

_____

_____

_____

_____

_____

SECTION 2: CONNECTION TO HATTIE'S EFFECT SIZES IN RELATION TO THE CORE COMPONENTS OF CHARACTER EDUCATION

Why Hattie's Effect Sizes?

In looking at what information about character education would be helpful for educators, we went back to the question of what works best in education. That question also drove Hattie's comprehensive meta-analysis of areas that contribute to learning: the student, the home, the school, the classroom, the curricula, the teacher, and teaching and learning approaches (Hattie, 2018). Along with providing information on the relative effects of these influences on student achievement, Hattie also emphasized the importance of understanding and making visible the story of the underlying data. One of his most critical findings was how important it is to make teaching and learning visible. We agree and feel the same about making the teaching and learning of *behavior* visible. We've compared key components of character education to influences Hattie identifies that impact student achievement. We feel these components are intrinsically linked to supporting a student's social emotional needs, and provide further evidence of the *why*; that is, implementation of these behavior initiatives is also critical to supporting a student's academic achievement. The following definition of key terms and description of how to interpret effect sizes will be a useful reference as you review the character education table in this section.

HOW TO INTERPRET EFFECT SIZES

Hattie's work is based on achievement outcomes, while this book focuses on behaviors. We know that misbehavior can take away from students' achievement outcomes. A 1.0 standard deviation is typically associated with an increase in student achievement by two to three years. An effect size of 1.0 would mean that, on average, students receiving that treatment would exceed 84 percent of students not receiving the treatment. Hattie (2009) sets the benchmark of an effect size of $d = 0.4$ as the "hinge-point" where anything above it is labeled in the "zone of desired effects" as influences with the greatest impact on student learning. That doesn't mean that anything below 0.4 shouldn't be explored in greater detail. It just means that the influences aren't as great. Effects between $d = 0.15$ and $d = 0.40$ are typically what teachers could accomplish across an ordinary year of teaching. Ninety-five percent of everything we do has a positive influence on achievement, so setting the benchmark at anything above zero would be pointless. Furthermore, the zone between $d = 0.0$ and $d = 0.15$ is what students could achieve without schooling or by the simple process of maturation alone. Therefore, any effects below $d = 0.15$ are potentially harmful and should not be implemented. The remaining 5 percent of the factors have reverse effects, or decrease achievement. To put it simply, Hattie (2009) says that "students who do not achieve at least 0.40 improvement in a year are going backwards" (p. 250). Additionally, "It is a teacher who does not achieve an average of $d > 0.40$ per year that I do not want my children to experience" (p. 126).

Hattie presents his research through seven main contributors to learning (referred to as sources of influence): *the student, curricula, home, school, classroom, teacher, and teaching and learning approaches.* Hattie works through each of these sources of influence to evaluate which specific innovations and influences (factors) have the greatest impact on achievement. The factors are grouped by more specific "aspects" of each source of influence.

Visualize it like this:

1. **Teaching: focus on implementation method (*source of influence*)**
   a. Implementation using out of school learning (*aspect*)
      i. Service learning (*factor*) (effect size [*d*] = 0.58)

2. **Curricula (*source of influence*)**
   a. Play programs (*aspect*)
      i. Social skills programs (*factor*) (*d* = 0.4)

The data in the table are listed from lowest effect size to highest. Remember, each source of influence is the broader category, and the subsets of each source are the aspects, which then group the various factors for each subset.

Character Education: Connection to Hattie's Effect Sizes in Relation to Core Components of This Behavior Initiative			
Source of Influence	**Aspect**	**Factor**	**Effect Size**
School	Leadership	School climate	0.32
Student	Physical influences	Drugs	0.32
Curricula	Other curricula programs	Motivation/character program	0.34
Classroom	Classroom influences	Decreasing disruptive behavior	0.34
Curricula	Play programs	Social skills programs	0.4
Classroom	Classroom influences	Classroom cohesion	0.44
Home	Family dynamics	Parental involvement	0.5
Home	Family dynamics	Home environment	0.52
Teacher	Teacher-student interactions	Teacher-student relationships	0.52
Teaching: focus on implementation method	Implementation using out of school learning	Service learning	0.58
Student	Motivation & mental state	Deep motivation and approach	0.69
Teaching: student learning strategies	Learning strategies	Effort	0.77
Teacher	Teacher attributes	Teacher credibility	0.9

Source: Hattie, J. (2018, October). *Visible Learning^plus 250+ influences on student achievement.* Retrieved from https://us.corwin.com/sites/default/files/250_influences_10.1.2018.pdf. Retrieved February 4, 2019.

Educators tend to focus on the influences that have the most positive effects on student learning (those at the bottom of the preceding list), using that information to decide what to do more of. They don't generally look at the top of the list to identify what to do less of. Understanding this list from a strength and deficit lens allows educators to become more cognizant of the factors they influence directly, allowing them to target the effects these influences have on learning (e.g., by continuing, decreasing, or ending altogether certain practices) in order to create environments that reverse negative effects and increase positive effects on student success.

For example, service learning has a 0.58 effect size on student achievement, which equates to over a year's growth in learning. Knowing the positive effect that service learning projects (out-of-school learning) have on student achievement, administrators can implement this type of teaching as a means of out-of-school learning to improve student achievement on their campus.

We encourage you to use this information to help guide implementation of behavior initiatives.

Section 2: Questions to Consider

What connections can you make between the effect sizes of the common components of implementation of character education and academic achievement?

_____

_____

_____

_____

_____

_____

_____

_____

_____

_____

_____

_____

How will you use effect sizes to ask questions that will allow you to dig deeper to improve practice?

_____

_____

_____

_____

_____

_____

_____

_____

_____

_____

_____

_____

How will you use this information with your colleagues to achieve the desired outcomes for students?

_____

_____

_____

_____

_____

_____

_____

_____

_____

_____

_____

_____

_____

_____

_____

_____

_____

_____

_____

_____

_____

_____

_____

_____

_____

_____

SECTION 3: SYNTHESIZED INDICATORS OF CHARACTER EDUCATION IMPLEMENTATION SUCCESS AND CHALLENGES

To develop this synthesized list of indicators of character education implementation success and challenges, we relied on our research and experiences as practitioners. Specifically, we used a combination of research and practices in the field based on our experiences as our reference to identify successes and challenges: peer-reviewed research study findings, practical application and experiences from the field, and expert testimonials to identify common implementation success trends and challenge trends. We wanted to provide this information as you consider implementation of this behavior initiative.

Character Education: Synthesized Indicators of Implementation Success and Challenges	
Implementation Success Trends	**Implementation Challenge Trends**
Implemented fully, faithfully, with fidelity	Incomplete or inaccurate implementation
Adequate professional development provided around implementation	Expensive professional development
Substantive support materials provided aligned with training experiences	Substantial time required for implementation and monitoring
Implementation approaches match school goals	Difficult to measure effectiveness
Success rises and falls on the shoulders of the administrators, especially the principal (for a school) or the superintendent (for a district)	Staff do not know how to implement components within their educational context
Adults modeling the character behaviors they expect from students	Difficult to embed in all topics; most often implemented in English language arts and history
Educational leaders need the same head, heart, and hand expected of students: they need to understand what quality character education is (the head); they need to commit to and deeply care about the character education and development of their students (the heart); and they need to model good character and practice quality character education as instructional leaders who know how to implement character education effectively (the hand)	Schools and districts need to prioritize professional development around character education
	Requires ongoing learning community structure, which is time consuming
Evaluation process in place to see if it is working	Does not provide a structure of how to utilize effectively with intensive behavior needs in students
Attention paid to school culture, including staff culture	Difficult to set up partnerships in the community
Also seen in the research showing that student perceptions of school as a caring community are critical to the effectiveness of character education	
Schools intentionally foster such bonding and monitor its development	
Takes at least three years to begin to make a positive impact on a schoolwide culture; substantial effects often seen only after five to seven years	
Many effective character education programs are bundles of component programs	
Include parents and other community representatives	
Includes role playing and skills training	
Explicit agenda	
Explicit that character is the focus, or make a focus on morality, values, virtues, or ethics explicit	
Community involvement	

Section 3: Question to Consider

To what extent will you use the synthesized indicators of implementation success and challenges to prevent obstacles during implementation?

_____

_____

_____

_____

_____

_____

_____

_____

_____

_____

_____

_____

_____

_____

_____

_____

_____

_____

_____

_____

_____

Character Education

SECTION 4: CHARACTER EDUCATION BEST-PRACTICE RESOURCE INVENTORY

To develop this best-practice resource inventory for character education implementation, we again used as our reference points a combination of research and best practices in the field based on our experiences. For example, we included effective resources based on (1) peer-reviewed research findings and (2) data from schools and districts implementing character education with effective outcomes for students. This information could be used as a starting point for looking into best-practice resources to assist with your implementation of character education. *Note*: We understand that other resources are available. What is provided here is what we found based on the aforementioned criteria for this best-practice resource inventory.

Character Education: Best-Practice Resource Inventory		
Resource	**Description** *Note:* **Some of the descriptions in this column are quoted directly from the listed resources.**	**References**
The 11 Principles of Effective Character Education	The 11 Principles of Effective Character Education are the cornerstone of the Character.org philosophy on effective character education. Each principle outlines vital aspects of character education initiatives that should not be overlooked in program implementation. From curriculum integration to extra-curricular activities, from parent and community partnerships to staff development—the 11 Principles of Effective Character Education offer fundamental guidance for educators and community leaders to maximize their character education outcomes.	character.org
CHARACTER COUNTS!	The Six Pillars of Character are the core ethical values of CHARACTER COUNTS! The six pillars are: Trustworthiness, Respect, Responsibility, Fairness, Caring, and Citizenship. CHARACTER COUNTS! recommends always using these pillars in this specific order and the use of the acronym of T.R.R.F.C.C. to help remember each pillar. Each Pillar is consistently identified with a color: Trustworthiness–Blue, Respect–Gold/Yellow, Responsibility–Green, Fairness–Orange, Caring–Red, Citizenship–Purple. Each of the six character traits are used within our CHARACTER COUNTS! program to help instill a positive school climate for students and a "culture of kindness," making schools a safe environment for students to learn.	https://charactercounts .org/program-overview/ six-pillars/
Peer Mediation	Peer mediation is problem solving by youth with youth. It is a process by which two or more students involved in a dispute meet in a private, safe, and confidential setting to work out problems with the assistance of a trained student mediator.	http://www.there solutioncenter.com/ peermediation/
Peers Making Peace Program	The only peer mediation program recognized by the U.S. Department of Education and the U.S. Department of Substance Abuse and listed on the Title IV Application, meaning it's approved for funding. Through the Peers Making Peace mediation program, young people can be empowered to resolve their own problems peacefully and improve their skills working with others. They have an opportunity to change the way they interact with each other and establish a new way of thinking about conflict, disputes, and differences.	http://www.theresolution center.com/peers -making-peace/
PRIMED Model	A Character Education framework designed to help implementation of effective character education in schools.	Berkowitz, Bier, and McCauley (2017)

Character Education: Best-Practice Resource Inventory		
Resource	**Description** *Note:* Some of the descriptions in this column are quoted directly from the listed resources.	**References**
Second Step	Second Step is a program rooted in social-emotional learning (SEL) that helps transform schools into supportive, successful learning environments uniquely equipped to help children thrive.	https://www.secondstep.org/
Open Circle Curriculum	During twice-weekly, 15-minute Open Circle Meetings . . . students form a circle of chairs, including an empty seat to symbolize that there is always room for another person, voice, or opinion.	https://www.open-circle.org/our-approach/curriculum
I Can Problem Solve (ICPS)	ICPS for Intermediate Elementary Grades contains 77 lessons. Based on 25 years of meticulous research, ICPS has proven to be extremely effective in helping children learn to resolve interpersonal problems and prevent antisocial behaviors. ICPS teaches children how to think, not what to think. It is a self-contained program that involves the use of games, stories, puppets, and role plays to make learning enjoyable. Each lesson contains a teacher script, reproducible illustrations, and a list of readily available materials.	http://www.icanproblemsolve.info/icps-for-intermediate-elementary-grades/
Guiding Good Choices (GGC), a modified version of the program formerly known as Preparing for the Drug Free Years	Guiding Good Choices (GGC) is a drug use prevention program that provides users with the knowledge and skills needed to guide children through early adolescence. It seeks to strengthen and clarify family expectations for behavior, enhance the conditions that promote bonding within the family, and teach skills that allow children to resist drug use successfully.	https://www.channing-bete.com/prevention-programs/guiding-good-choices/guiding-good-choices.html
Life Skills Training Program	Life Skills Training Program covers social skills, including using verbal and non-verbal communication cues to avoid misunderstandings.	https://www.lifeskillstraining.com/training-overview/
CharacterPlus	The CharacterPlus Way is an important part of a successful character education program, which we implement in district or individual schools during a three-year process. This district-wide evidence-based school reform program develops a healthy school culture using data driven planning, intrinsic student motivation and collaborative classroom practices.	https://characterplus.org/
Building Decision Skills	Building Decision Skills provides an interactive model for teaching ethics in the classroom. Aims to raise middle and high school students' awareness of ethics, help them gain practical experience in developing core values, and give them practical strategies for dealing with ethical dilemmas. Building Decision Skills consists of 10 lessons that can fill two consecutive weeks of daily lessons or be drawn out over a longer period. Using readings, handouts, and overheads, the teacher covers key concepts. Students are encouraged to think about the key concepts through small-group activities, class discussions, and homework assignments. The program also includes schoolwide components (such as group discussions, seminars, and assemblies). And it can be combined with service learning.	www.globalethics.org/services/edu/bds.htm
Caring School Community (CSC), a modified version of a program formerly known as the Child Development Project	*CSC* is a multiyear school improvement program that involves all students in grades K–6. The program aims to promote core values, prosocial behavior, and a schoolwide feeling of community. The program consists of four elements originally developed for the *Child Development Project*: class meeting lessons, cross-age "buddies" programs, "homeside" activities, and schoolwide community.	https://www.collaborativeclassroom.org/programs/caring-school-community/

(Continued)

Character Education: Best-Practice Resource Inventory (Continued)		
Resource	**Description** *Note:* Some of the descriptions in this column are quoted directly from the listed resources.	**References**
Teaching Students to be Peacemakers (TSP)	The Teaching Students to be Peacemakers (TSP) program was designed to target conflict resolution and mediation behaviors in elementary school-aged children. Students in the program receive up to nine hours of peer-mediation training over several weeks. The program evaluation, which randomly assigned classrooms, found that the program was effective in teaching children more constructive negotiation strategies for dealing with conflict.	http://www.co-operation.org/
Facing History and Ourselves	Facing History and Ourselves is a secondary program designed to help integrate the study of history, literature, and human behavior as it relates to ethical decision making, historical understanding, social-emotional learning, and critical thinking. Helps students make connections to history and learn how to make a difference in the world.	https://www.facinghistory.org/
Peaceful Schools	In the Peaceful Schools Project students are taught relaxation exercises to help manage stress and anger. Peaceful Schools seeks to develop character and social skills in youth and prevent acts of violence in educational settings. The Peaceful Schools Model works toward curbing problem behaviors and developing social competence in order to prevent youth violence and create positive, productive school climates.	http://peacefulschools.com/
Building Moral Intelligence: The Seven Essential Virtues That Teach Kids to Do the Right Thing	Gain a new understanding of moral intelligence and a step-by-step program for its achievement from bestselling author Michele Borba. In this indispensable book for parents, Borba has created a new breakthrough in conceptualizing and teaching virtue, character, and values under the auspices of a measurable capacity—Moral Intelligence. This book confronts the front-page crisis we now face in our country regarding youth violence, alienation, self-destructive behavior, cold-heartedness, lack of compassion, insensitivity, intolerance, and the breakdown of values. The author provides a new way to understand, evaluate, and inspire our kids with the seven essential virtues which comprise moral intelligence.	Borba (2002)
The Center for Character & Citizenship	The Center for Character & Citizenship, co-directed by Marvin W. Berkowitz and Melinda C. Bier, is designed around research and advocacy of character education. The center provides resources and toolkits to assist educators about character and citizenship education. Some of the programs and resources highlighted include Leadership Academy in Character Education, Youth Empowerment in Action!, and the Journal of Character Education.	https://characterandcitizenship.org/

Section 4: Questions to Consider

What resources do you think would help with your implementation of this behavior initiative?

_____

_____

_____

_____

_____

_____

_____

_____

_____

Name one resource listed that you will investigate further and why.

_____

_____

_____

_____

_____

_____

_____

_____

_____

_____

Character Education

RESTORATIVE JUSTICE

IN THIS CHAPTER you will find information on restorative justice divided into four sections, each followed by questions to consider to help you evaluate this behavior initiative and guide meaningful discussions around possible implementation in your school or district.

Section 1: The *What*—Restorative Justice

Section 2: Connection to Hattie's Effect Sizes in Relation to the Core Components of Restorative Justice

Section 3: Synthesized Indicators of Restorative Justice Implementation Success and Challenges

Section 4: Restorative Justice Best-Practice Resource Inventory

SECTION 1: THE *WHAT*—RESTORATIVE JUSTICE

Every student has a story but sometimes their behavior doesn't allow us time to hear their story. The goal of using restorative practices is to give educators the time to hear a student, understand a student, and then create the appropriate and equal response for that student. Our goal is for our students to understand their impact and be able to repair harm as needed.

Restorative practices are not a program but rather a mindset shift to help support the growth of students. Our goal is to allow students to learn from their mistakes. We believe in holding our students accountable and finding a restorative outcome rather than a punitive consequence.

Student and teacher relationships are one of the most important elements in education. With restorative practices we believe that students will second-guess their choices, not because they are breaking the rules but, rather, because they are hurting the relationship they have with an adult.

—Dominique Smith

Coauthor, *Better Than Carrots or Sticks*

Simply put, restorative justice is a structure designed to shift mindsets from punitive to restorative, improve relationships, and repair and learn from injustices. However, there are some noteworthy variations in common restorative justice definitions and styles of implementation. Even given the variations, the intended outcomes for restorative justice implementation are similar.

Each chapter in Part II is divided into four sections that end with questions to help guide discussions with your teacher or leadership teams around each behavior initiative. As you navigate through this chapter, remember to use the Behavior Initiatives K-W-L strategy to help organize your learnings around restorative justice implementation, beginning with the purpose for implementing restorative justice and common definitions (i.e., the *what*).

Purpose for Restorative Justice

- Create a positive school culture
- Reduce suspensions, expulsions, and disciplinary referrals
- Shift from punishment to compassion (punitive to restorative)
- Shift adult mindsets about discipline
- Value establishing relationships
- Value repairing relationships
- Encourage student voice
- Give victims a greater voice in the criminal justice system
- Allow victims to receive an explanation and more meaningful reparation from offenders
- Make offenders accountable by allowing them to take responsibility for their actions
- Build community confidence that offenders are making amends for their wrongdoing
- Improve communication and school connections for both students and family
- Effectively address behavior and other complex school issues
- Offer a supportive environment that can improve learning

- Improve safety by preventing future harm
- Offer alternatives to suspensions and expulsions
- Support conflict-resolution and critical-thinking skills
- Develop valuable skills among students for college and employment beyond school
- Promote fairness

Variations of Restorative Justice

Based on our experiences helping schools implement behavior initiatives and through our research findings, we have noticed that there are multiple definitions or variations of each of the six behavior initiatives outlined in this book. That can be overwhelming while you are trying to decide which behavior initiative is best for your school or district, so we outline three common definitions for each of the six behavior initiatives identified in this book, based on repeated mentions of them through the research and in the field. *Note:* If a definition you prefer is not cited in this section, it does not mean it is not a worthy definition to use. We just want to provide a few examples of common definitions to help educators better understand each behavior initiative. We strongly believe that school or district staff need to understand the *what* definition and the rest of the information in each of these chapters in order to make informed decisions about implementation.

THREE COMMON RESTORATIVE JUSTICE DEFINITIONS

Common Definition 1: "Restorative justice is an evidence-based practice effectively used to reduce suspensions, expulsions, and disciplinary referrals. Restorative justice focuses on righting a wrong committed and repairing harm done. The goal is to place value on relationships and focus on repairing relationships that have been injured. The victim and the wrongdoer have the opportunity to share with one another how they were harmed, as victims, or how they will work to resolve the harm caused, as wrongdoers" (Anderson et al., 2014, p. 3).

Common Definition 2: "Restorative justice is a fundamental change in how you respond to rule violations and misbehavior. Restorative justice resolves disciplinary problems in a cooperative and constructive way" (Claassen & Claassen, 2008).

Common Definition 3: "Restorative justice is a philosophy based on a set of principles that guide the response to conflict and harm. These principles are based on practices that have been used for centuries in indigenous cultures and religious groups." Restorative justice's three main goals are accountability, community safety, and competency and development (Ashley & Burke, 2009):

- *Accountability.* Restorative justice strategies provide opportunities for wrongdoers to be accountable to those they have harmed, and enable them to repair the harm they caused to the extent possible.

- *Community safety.* Restorative justice recognizes the need to keep the community safe through strategies that build relationships and empower the community to take responsibility for the well-being of its members.

- *Competency development.* Restorative justice seeks to increase the pro-social skills of those who have harmed others, address underlying factors that lead youth to engage in delinquent behavior, and build on strengths in each young person.

In Chapter 1 of this book, we shared a snapshot of a restorative justice school as a reference. We also want to provide a before-and-after story to help reinforce the beliefs and behaviors necessary for implementing restorative justice in your school or district.

A BEFORE-AND-AFTER RESTORATIVE JUSTICE STORY

Before restorative justice . . . we considered ourselves a zero-tolerance school and were embarrassingly proud of it. Teachers used detentions and suspensions as their only means of discipline at the school. We experienced fights on campus every week. Oftentimes, the school officer was involved with the fights, especially the ones that included a weapon of some sort and the students were removed from the classroom and school setting and transported to juvenile hall, without being given the opportunity to restore any injustices or learn from their behaviors. Charges were always pressed, and the perception was that if we got them off our campus, our school would be safer. As a result, we had the highest number of suspensions and expulsions in the district, drug dogs were a regular sight on campus, and the community was pushing for metal detectors and additional school officers on campus. It always felt as if we were being reactionary and punitive rather than preventive and supportive.

After restorative justice . . . we struggled at first with the misconceptions that nothing was happening about discipline at our school anymore due to these alternative discipline practices. However, we started seeing students respond to a more supportive and preventive approach, resulting in less repeated offenses. We also started noticing that families were more willing to work with us when they did not feel as if we were throwing away or giving up on their children. The buy-in from the staff improved over time; however, it required modeling and support from administration. The buy-in from students also improved because they felt as if the adults were actually there to support them and help them if they were struggling with a situation. Resources were invested in more social workers and intervention support providers rather than metal detectors and school officers. Having these additional resources helping to connect with students and providing opportunities to restore relationships between students and teachers made a huge impact. Teachers no longer resorted to detentions and suspensions as the only means of responding to students. They took more time in getting to know the students and working with them on how to resolve issues rather than making it someone else's problem. Fights decreased, and students actually felt safer as a result of knowing their teachers and the staff cared about them.

Section 1: Questions to Consider

What are the intended outcomes of your school's or district's restorative justice initiative?

_____

_____

_____

_____

_____

_____

_____

_____

_____

How does your school or district define restorative justice?

_____
_____
_____
_____
_____
_____
_____
_____

What is currently in place at your school or district?

_____
_____
_____
_____
_____
_____
_____
_____

What would your next steps be, given what you have read so far?

_____
_____
_____
_____
_____
_____
_____
_____
_____

Restorative Justice

SECTION 2: CONNECTION TO HATTIE'S EFFECT SIZES IN RELATION TO THE CORE COMPONENTS OF RESTORATIVE JUSTICE

Why Hattie's Effect Sizes?

In looking at what information about restorative justice would be helpful for educators, we went back to the question of what works best in education. That question also drove Hattie's comprehensive meta-analysis of areas that contribute to learning: the student, the home, the school, the classroom, the curricula, the teacher, and teaching and learning approaches (Hattie, 2018). Along with providing information on the relative effects of these influences on student achievement, Hattie also emphasized the importance of understanding and making visible the story of the underlying data. One of his most critical findings was how important it is to make teaching and learning visible. We agree and feel the same about making the teaching and learning of *behavior* visible. We've compared key components of restorative justice to influences Hattie identifies that impact student achievement. We feel these components are intrinsically linked to supporting a student's social emotional needs, and provide further evidence of the *why*; that is, implementation of these behavior initiatives is also critical to supporting a student's academic achievement. The following definition of key terms and description of how to interpret effect sizes will be a useful reference as you review the restorative justice table in this section.

HOW TO INTERPRET EFFECT SIZES

Hattie's work is based on achievement outcomes, while this book focuses on behaviors. We know that misbehavior can take away from students' achievement outcomes. A 1.0 standard deviation is typically associated with an increase in student achievement by two to three years. An effect size of 1.0 would mean that, on average, students receiving that treatment would exceed 84 percent of students not receiving the treatment. Hattie (2009) sets the benchmark of an effect size of $d = 0.4$ as the "hinge-point" where anything above it is labeled in the "zone of desired effects" as influences with the greatest impact on student learning. That doesn't mean that anything below 0.4 shouldn't be explored in greater detail. It just means that the influences aren't as great. Effects between $d = 0.15$ and $d = 0.40$ are typically what teachers could accomplish across an ordinary year of teaching. Ninety-five percent of everything we do has a positive influence on achievement, so setting the benchmark at anything above zero would be pointless. Furthermore, the zone between $d = 0.0$ and $d = 0.15$ is what students could achieve without schooling or by the simple process of maturation alone. Therefore, any effects below $d = 0.15$ are potentially harmful and should not be implemented. The remaining 5 percent of the factors have reverse effects, or decrease achievement. To put it simply, Hattie (2009) says that "students who do not achieve at least 0.40 improvement in a year are going backwards" (p. 250). Additionally, "It is a teacher who does not achieve an average of $d > 0.40$ per year that I do not want my children to experience" (p. 126).

Hattie presents his research through seven main contributors to learning (referred to as sources of influence): *the student, curricula, home, school, classroom, teacher, and teaching and learning approaches.* Hattie works through each of these sources of influence to evaluate which specific innovations and influences (factors) have the greatest impact on achievement. The factors are grouped by more specific "aspects" of each source of influence.

Visualize it like this:

1. **Classroom (*source of influence*)**
   a. Classroom influences (*aspect*)
      i. Classroom cohesion (*factor*) (effect size [*d*] = 0.44)

2. **Teacher (*source of influence*)**
   a. Teacher-student interactions (*aspect*)
      i. Teacher-student relationships (*factor*) (*d* = 0.52)

The data in the table are listed from lowest effect size to highest. Remember, each source of influence is the broader category, and the subsets of each source are the aspects, which then group the various factors for each subset.

Restorative Justice: Connection to Hattie's Effect Sizes in Relation to the Core Components of This Behavior Initiative			
Source of Influence	**Aspect**	**Factor**	**Effect Size**
Home	Family dynamics	Corporal punishment in the home	−0.33
School	Other school effects	Suspending or expelling students	−0.2
School	Leadership	School climate	0.32
Student	Beliefs, attitudes, dispositions	Stereotype threat	0.33
Classroom	Classroom influences	Decreasing disruptive behavior	0.34
Classroom	Classroom influences	Classroom management	0.35
Student	Beliefs, attitudes, dispositions	Self-concept	0.41
Classroom	Classroom influences	Classroom cohesion	0.44
Teacher	Teacher-student interactions	Teacher-student relationships	0.52
Classroom	Classroom influences	Peer influences	0.53
Teaching: focus on implementation method	Implementation using out of school learning	Service learning	0.58
Classroom	Classroom influences	Classroom behavioral	0.62
Teacher	Teacher attributes	Teacher credibility	0.9

Source: Hattie, J. (2018, October). *Visible Learning^plus^ 250+ influences on student achievement.* Retrieved from https://us.corwin.com/sites/default/files/250_influences_10.1.2018.pdf. Retrieved February 4, 2019.

Educators tend to focus on the influences that have the most positive effects on student learning (those at the bottom of the preceding list), using that information to decide what to do more of. They don't generally look at the top of the list to identify what to do less of. Understanding this list from a strength and deficit lens allows educators to become more cognizant of the factors they influence directly, allowing them to target the effects these influences have on learning (e.g., by continuing, decreasing, or ending altogether certain practices) in order to create environments that reverse negative effects and increase positive effects on student success.

For example, the aspect of beliefs, attitudes, and dispositions within the factor of self-concept has a positive effect size of 0.41 on student achievement, which equates to a year's growth in learning. Additionally, teacher-student interactions/relationships has a positive effect size of 0.52. Knowing the positive effect both have on student achievement, administrators and teachers can create environments that build students' beliefs in who they are and daily conditions so that students know they are in the presence of caring adults who have their best interests at heart.

We encourage you to use this information to help guide implementation of behavior initiatives.

Section 2: Questions to Consider

What connections can you make between the effect sizes of the common components of implementation of restorative justice and academic achievement?

_____

_____

_____

_____

_____

_____

_____

_____

_____

How will you use effect sizes to ask questions that will allow you to dig deeper to improve practice?

_____

_____

_____

_____

_____

_____

_____

_____

_____

_____

How will you use this information with your colleagues to achieve the desired outcomes for students?

_____

_____

_____

_____

_____

_____

_____

_____

_____

_____

_____

_____

_____

_____

_____

_____

_____

_____

_____

_____

_____

_____

_____

_____

_____

Restorative Justice

SECTION 3: SYNTHESIZED INDICATORS OF RESTORATIVE JUSTICE IMPLEMENTATION SUCCESS AND CHALLENGES

To develop this synthesized list of indicators of restorative justice implementation success and challenges, we relied on our research and experiences as practitioners. Specifically, we used a combination of peer-reviewed research findings, practical application and experiences from the field, and expert testimonials as our reference to identify common implementation success trends and challenge trends. We wanted to provide this information as you consider implementation of this behavior initiative.

Restorative Justice: Synthesized Indicators of Implementation Success and Challenges	
Implementation Success Trends	**Implementation Challenge Trends**
Monitored implementation	Time and funding (e.g., training, teachers' overtime, recognitions and awards, and marketing materials)
Administrator buy-in	
Staff embracing a change	Takes time to implement any new practice fully (3–5 years)
Treating students fairly	
Leadership	Lack of staff and student training
Offering professional development in RJ philosophy and practices for all staff including those in nonteaching roles	Moving from theory to practice
	Beliefs of the adults
Embed restorative justice approaches with the students including training	Poor overall school culture
	Not always formalized
Direct sanctions needed as a backup if the restorative process fails	Sustainability
	Hard paradigm shift
Active student voice and student feedback	School structures not designed to support restorative justice practices
Include skill building	Poor communication and messaging
Develop and maintain a cohort of highly skilled facilitators	Lack of student ownership
	Limited resources
Developing state and school policies that include restorative justice	Fears of violence
	Competing initiatives
Supporting restorative justice philosophy and practice through teacher education	School resources are driven by academic state test scores
	Restorative seen as lenient on students who break rules
	Traditional mindset about discipline difficult to change

Section 3: Question to Consider

To what extent will you use the synthesized indicators of implementation success and challenges to prevent obstacles during implementation?

_____

_____

_____

_____

_____

_____

_____

_____

_____

_____

_____

_____

_____

_____

_____

_____

_____

_____

_____

_____

_____

_____

_____

Restorative Justice

SECTION 4: RESTORATIVE JUSTICE BEST-PRACTICE RESOURCE INVENTORY

To develop this best-practice resource inventory for restorative justice implementation, we again used as our reference points a combination of research and best practices in the field based on our experiences. For example, we included effective resources based on (1) peer-reviewed research findings and (2) data from schools and districts implementing restorative justice with effective outcomes for students. This information could be used as a starting point for looking into best-practice resources to assist with your implementation of restorative justice. *Note:* We understand that other resources are available. What is provided here is what we found based on the aforementioned criteria for this best-practice resource inventory.

Restorative Justice: Best-Practice Resource Inventory		
Resource	**Description** *Note:* Some of the descriptions in this column are quoted directly from the listed resources.	**References**
Victim Offender Mediation	Victim Offender Mediation, also referred to as VOM, involves active involvement by the victim and the offender, giving them the opportunity to mutually rectify the harm done to the victim in a process that promotes dialogue between them. This resource is part of the Centre for Justice and Reconciliation, which provides resources and programs for educators and the community on restorative justice.	http://restorativejustice .org/restorative-justice/ about-restorative -justice/tutorial-intro -to-restorative-justice/ lesson-3-programs/ victim-offender -mediation/#sthash .i9ekOwT3.dpbs
Better Than Carrots or Sticks	Restorative justice is also implemented directly in classrooms, in the form of "circles" in which students talk through problems before they get out of hand.	Smith, Fisher, and Frey (2015)
Community Group Conferencing	For more serious offenses, a conference between parents, victims, offenders, other affected staff and students (and sometimes law enforcement) to discuss the offense. Conferencing opens the process to other students, staff, and teachers to work with affected parties to develop an appropriate response to the conflict.	Bazemore and Umbreit (2001)
Circle Processes	The circle process is based on indigenous practice that value inclusiveness, respect, dealing with things as a community and supporting healing. Open, facilitated discussion about a specific incident or general issue the community needs to address.	http://restorative solutions.us/resources/ resources-and-links -handouts
Don't Suspend Me! An Alternative Discipline Toolkit	*Don't Suspend Me!* gives educators the tools they need to apply alternative discipline methods. Includes a toolkit with alternative strategies to use for the most common behavior challenges and worksheets and exercises for the major discipline incidents that occur in schools throughout the nation.	Hannigan and Hannigan (2017)
Restorative Conference	A restorative conference is a structured meeting between offenders, victims and both parties' family and friends, in which they deal with the consequences of the crime or wrongdoing and decide how best to repair the harm. Neither a counseling nor a mediation process, conferencing is a victim-sensitive, straightforward problem-solving method that demonstrates how citizens can resolve their own problems when provided with a constructive forum to do so (O'Connell, Wachtel, & Wachtel, 1999).	https://www.iirp.edu/ defining-restorative/ restorative-conference

Restorative Justice: Best-Practice Resource Inventory		
Resource	**Description** *Note:* **Some of the descriptions in this column are quoted directly from the listed resources.**	**References**
Classroom and Peace-Keeping Circles	Discuss class issues/harm within class or problems affecting students in general. Incident and other issues may be addressed as needed. Can be on-going. Face to face, in circle, with a talking piece and trained circle keeper. Principles for forming circles in classrooms include: • Practice giving and receiving compliments, • Create a student-generated agenda, foster good communication skills, • Learn, understand, and respect differences, • Explore reasons for why people do what they do, • Practice role-playing and brainstorming to solve problems, • Focus on non-punitive solutions, and • Ensure confidentiality among participants.	http://peaceofthecircle .com/trainings/
Peer Mediation	Involves trained peer mediators who assist their peers in settling disputes. Students are trained in peer mediation strategies and apply restorative-problem solving techniques.	http://www.brockton publicschools.com/ uploaded/Programs -Services/Health Educatioon/Peer -Mediation/elem-peer -mediation.pdf
Conflict Resolution and Skill Building	Learning process that helps individuals understand conflict dynamics, empowers them to use communication and creative thinking to build relationships, and to fairly and peacefully manage and resolve conflict. Conflict resolution programs provide students with problem-solving and self-control skills. These programs teach young people how to manage potential conflict, defuse situations, assuage hurt feelings, and reduce any inclination to retaliate after a conflict. Conflict resolution programs walk students through their emotions in the presence of one another and guide them through a team process of addressing the issues that gave rise to the conflict in the first instance. Because conflict resolution addresses and works to resolve the root causes of conflict, it helps prevent future incidents from occurring.	https://www.ncjrs.gov/ pdffiles/conflic.pdf https://restorativejustice .org.uk/sites/default/ files/resources/files/ Practitioners%20 Handbook_0.pdf
Responsive Classroom Morning Meetings	Morning Meeting is an engaging way to start each day, build a strong sense of community, and set children up for success socially and academically. Each morning, students and teachers gather together in a circle for twenty to thirty minutes and interact with one another during four purposeful components: 1. Greeting: Students and teachers greet one other by name. 2. Sharing: Students share information about important events in their lives. Listeners often offer empathetic comments or ask clarifying questions.	https://www .responsiveclassroom .org/about/principles -practices/

(Continued)

Restorative Justice

Restorative Justice: Best-Practice Resource Inventory (Continued)		
Resource	**Description** *Note:* **Some of the descriptions in this column are quoted directly from the listed resources.**	**References**
	3. Group Activity: Everyone participates in a brief, lively activity that fosters group cohesion and helps students practice social and academic skills (for example, reciting a poem, dancing, singing, or playing a game). 4. Morning Message: Students read and interact with a short message written by their teacher. The message is crafted to help students focus on the work they'll do in school that day. **Morning Meeting**—Everyone in the classroom gathers in a circle for twenty to thirty minutes at the beginning of each school day and proceeds through four sequential components: greeting, sharing, group activity, and morning message. **Responsive Advisory Meeting**—A routine that builds positive, meaningful relationships with caring adults and peers. Components: arrival welcome, announcements, acknowledgements, and activity.	
Classroom Respect Agreements	Children play an integral part of their classroom culture. They and their teacher create a classroom agreement and all agree to be accountable. Together they determine how they will treat each other and create a positive classroom community.	Claasen and Claasen (2008)
Peacemaking Circles or Healing Circles	Circles have a wide array of uses and purposes both in and out of the juvenile justice system. They can be used as a practice in schools and communities for building relationships and changing community cultures as well as a community-directed process, conducted in partnership with the justice system, to develop consensus on an appropriate plan that addresses the concerns of all those affected by a crime. Circles use traditional circle ritual and structure to involve the victim, victim supporters, the offender, offender supporters, justice personnel, police, and all interested community members. Within the circle, people can speak from the heart in a shared search for understanding of the event, and together identify the steps necessary to assist in healing all affected parties and prevent future crimes.	http://ibarji.org/circles.asp
Sentencing Circles	The procedure is as straightforward as the name suggests. Everyone in the community is invited to attend and participate. Chairs are arranged in a circle and the session is chaired either by a respected member of the community, sometimes called "the keeper of the circle" or by the judge. Usually between 15 and 50 persons are in attendance. The participants in the circle introduce themselves, then the charges are read and the Crown and defense lawyers make brief opening remarks. The community members then speak. A justice system professional participating in a circle for the first time may wonder about the relevance of much of what is said during a circle sentencing. Unlike a formal court-based sentencing, the discussions focus on more than just the offence and the offender and often include the following matters: • The extent of similar crimes within the community; • The underlying cause of such crimes;	https://www.iirp.edu/eforum-archive/circle-sentencing-part-of-the-restorative-justice-continuum

Restorative Justice: Best-Practice Resource Inventory		
Resource	**Description** *Note:* Some of the descriptions in this column are quoted directly from the listed resources.	**References**
	• A retrospective analysis of what life in the community had been before crime became so prevalent; • The impact of these sorts of crimes on victims generally, on families and community life and the impact of this crime on the victim; • What can be done within the community to prevent this type of dysfunctional behavior; • What must be done to help heal the offender, the victim and the community; • What will constitute the sentence plan; • Who will be responsible for carrying out the plan, and who will support the offender and victim in ensuring the plan is successfully implemented; • A date to review the sentence and a set of goals to be achieved before review.	
Community Service/ Restitution	Community service allows for individuals to restore a harm they may have committed to the school community by providing a meaningful service that contributes to their individual improvement. Restorative Community Service is service done by the offender that is restorative in nature and intent. Restorative Community Service includes the offender in choosing what the repair/activity will be. It is not assigned without their consent. This service is typically done for or at the request of the victim or another circle participant who was harmed by the incident and/or is community service that uses and strengthens the assets of the offender and is intended to benefit him/her in addition to benefiting the community.	Restorative Justice Colorado (2014)
Peer Jury (sometimes called teen court, youth court, or peer court)	A youth centered program in which student volunteers hear cases of minor delinquent acts or school offenses. Peer juries are overseen by an adult coordinator with youth volunteers acting as jurors. Police departments, community agencies, probation departments, and schools can coordinate peer jury programs.	http://www.icjia.state .il.us/assets/pdf/BARJ/ SCHOOL%20BARJ%20 GUIDEBOOOK.pdf
Restorative Contracts or Restorative Repairs	A behavioral contract in which the student and teacher or staff collaborate on a solution, giving the student ownership of future consequences to his behavior. The outcome of the conference is a contract that the offender must comply with. The contract typically consists of a number of actions or items that must be completed in a certain period of time. These contracts typically include some of the following requirements: letters of apology, community service, financial restitution, counseling, and report writing. Each contract is dependent on the crime committed and the requests of the victim. In a case where the contract is not completed, the offender will be referred back to the traditional system, where criminal charges will be filed, starting the retributive justice process. If the offender completes the contract within the specified amount of time, the offense will never appear as a criminal violation on their official record.	Riley (2017); Restorative Justice Colorado (2014)

(Continued)

Restorative Justice: Best-Practice Resource Inventory (Continued)		
Resource	**Description** *Note:* Some of the descriptions in this column are quoted directly from the listed resources.	**References**
	These are potential agreement/contract items that are often included in restorative justice practices. They are neither restorative justice nor a restorative practice in and of themselves. The possibilities for restorative repairs go well beyond this list. The repair of harm should be determined by a group that includes harmed parties, people responsible for harm and community representatives. In some restorative practices, repairs may be categorically pre-determined to create efficiencies of process. In all cases, repairs should be specific to the incident and the person responsible, build on their strengths, and repair harm. If the repairs are punitive, they are not restorative. These include but are not limited to: • Restitution • Apologies • Meaningful/Restorative Community Service • Educational Opportunities	
Restorative ReEntry Circles/Transition Circles	Restorative ReEntry Circles/Transition Circles are provided for imprisoned individuals who are returning to a community. The person returning to life outside of incarceration will meet with community members, their families and friends in a group process to address their needs for a successful transition back into the community.	Bazemore and Stinchcomb (2004)

Section 4: Questions to Consider

What resources do you think would help with your implementation of this behavior initiative?

_____

_____

_____

_____

_____

_____

_____

_____

_____

Name one resource listed that you will investigate further and why.

_____

_____

_____

_____

_____

_____

_____

_____

_____

_____

_____

_____

_____

_____

_____

_____

_____

_____

_____

_____

_____

_____

_____

_____

_____

CULTURALLY
RESPONSIVE TEACHING

Section 1: The *What*—Culturally Responsive Teaching (CRT)

Section 2: Connection to Hattie's Effect Sizes in Relation to the Core Components of CRT

Section 3: Synthesized Indicators of CRT Implementation Success and Challenges

Section 4: CRT Best-Practice Resource Inventory

SECTION 1: THE *WHAT*—CULTURALLY RESPONSIVE TEACHING (CRT)

The essence of culturally responsive teaching can be expressed in the following six statements:

1. The more culturally competent and responsive I am in my classroom, the more I can come to know who my students really are.

2. The more I know my students, the better I can shift my practice to be meaningful for them.

3. The more meaningful my teaching is for them, the greater will be their willingness and capacity to invest in the learning process.

4. The greater their willingness to authentically engage, the greater will be their academic success and life chances.

5. The more real and refined I become in my culturally responsive pedagogy, the less pressure my students feel to either conform or assimilate to dominant culture expectations.

6. The less pressure they feel to assimilate, the more we begin to unravel the deleterious effects of past and current oppression.

There is no work more complex than culturally responsive teaching, and there is no work more important.

—Gary Howard
Author, *We Can't Teach What We Don't Know*

Simply put, culturally responsive teaching (CRT) is a structure designed to empower students to have a voice in their learning and be taught in a way that is meaningful for them as it relates to their culture and current context. However, there are some noteworthy variations in common CRT definitions and styles of implementation. Even given the variations, the intended outcomes for CRT implementation are similar.

Each chapter in Part II is divided into four sections that end with questions to help guide discussions with your teacher or leadership teams around each behavior initiative. As you navigate through this chapter, remember to use the Behavior Initiatives K-W-L strategy to help organize your learnings around CRT implementation, beginning with the purpose for implementing CRT and common definitions (i.e., the *what*).

Purpose for CRT

- Create a positive school culture
- Recognize the importance of including students' cultural references in all aspects of learning
- Build resilience and growth mindsets
- Establish positive perspectives on parents and families
- Have and hold high expectations for all students
- Establish an environment in which students learn within the context of culture

- Provide student-centered and teacher-facilitated instruction
- Reshape traditional curriculum
- Teach in a way that respects culture, language, and racial identity
- Build students' learning capacity

- Develop students with a critical lens for injustices
- Create an environment that celebrates diversity of cultures
- Teaching pedagogy grounded in teachers displaying cultural competence
- Develop students' critical thinking skills

Variations of CRT

Based on our experiences helping schools implement behavior initiatives and through our research findings, we have noticed that there are multiple definitions or variations of the six behavior initiatives outlined in this book. That can be overwhelming while you are trying to decide which behavior initiative is best for your school or district, so we outline three common definitions for each of the six behavior initiatives identified in this book, based on repeated mentions of them through the research and in the field. *Note:* If a definition you prefer is not cited in this section, it does not mean it is not a worthy definition to use. We just want to provide a few examples of common definitions to help educators better understand each behavior initiative. We strongly believe that school or district staff need to understand the *what* definition and the rest of the information in each of these chapters in order to make informed decisions about implementation.

THREE COMMON CRT DEFINITIONS

Common Definition 1: The term *culturally responsive teaching* (CRT) originated decades ago when Gloria Ladson-Billings (1994) used it to describe "a pedagogy that empowers students intellectually, socially, emotionally, and politically by using cultural references to impart knowledge, skills, and attitudes" (p. 20).
Characteristics of CRT are

1. Positive perspectives on parents and families
2. Communication of high expectations
3. Learning within the context of culture
4. Student-centered instruction
5. Culturally mediated instruction
6. Reshaping the curriculum
7. Teacher as facilitator

Common Definition 2: Howard (2016) outlines seven principles for culturally responsive teaching:

1. Students are affirmed in their cultural connections
2. Teachers are personally inviting
3. Learning environments are physically and culturally inviting

(Continued)

(Continued)

4. Students are reinforced for academic development

5. Instructional changes are made to accommodate differences in learners

6. Classroom is managed with firm, consistent, loving control

7. Instruction stresses collectivity as well as individuality

Common Definition 3: Culturally responsive teaching is defined by Gay (2010) as "using the cultural characteristics, experiences, and perspectives of ethnically diverse students as conduits for teaching them more effectively. It is based on the assumption that when academic knowledge and skills are situated within the lived experiences and frames of reference of students, they are more personally meaningful, have higher interest appeal, and are learned more easily and thoroughly" (p. 106).

Essential elements of CRT are

1. Developing a cultural diversity knowledge base

2. Designing culturally relevant curricula

3. Demonstrating cultural caring and building a learning community

4. Cross-cultural communications

5. Cultural congruity in classroom instruction

In Chapter 1 of this book, we shared a snapshot of a CRT school as a reference. We also want to provide a before-and-after story to help reinforce the beliefs and behaviors necessary for implementing CRT in your school or district.

A BEFORE-AND-AFTER CRT STORY

Before CRT . . . teachers were publicly complaining about how the boundary changes in the district resulted in an entirely new group of students who were behavior problems at their school. Suspensions and expulsions tripled within the first month of the new school year. Many veteran teachers put in for transfers to other schools. Teachers and administrators were afraid to speak to "the new parents" who were from the apartment buildings because they felt as if they were loud and aggressive. As a result, no connections or relationships were made, and misconceptions about each other continued to grow. Students and community members felt they were not welcomed at the school and as a result did not want to be involved with the school. Teachers blamed the parents for these behaviors and spoke poorly about them. Three different administrators were cycled through the school in the first two years after these boundary changes. Everyone was frustrated and did not know how to improve the school culture.

After CRT . . . teachers were able to understand cultural differences between themselves and their diverse group of students. The classroom environment was designed so that teachers and students could appreciate different cultures and learn from them across the curriculum. High expectations were set for students, and teacher excuses for poor performance were not accepted. Teachers made an intentional effort to connect with the parents and work with them to help the students in their classrooms learn and behave. Efforts were made regularly to improve the school and community relationships. Students began to feel as if their teachers understood them and where they were coming from rather than trying to change them and not accept them for who they were. Behavior began to improve and teachers felt more supported at the school. The teachers agreed to a norm that they would not speak poorly about students, their parents, or the community amongst themselves or with others (i.e., the expectation was understood by staff; negative comments would not be tolerated).

Section 1: Questions to Consider

What are the intended outcomes of your school's or district's CRT initiative?

_____

_____

_____

_____

_____

_____

_____

_____

_____

_____

How does your school or district define CRT?

_____

_____

_____

_____

_____

_____

_____

_____

_____

_____

_____

_____

Culturally Responsive Teaching

(Continued)

(Continued)

What is currently in place at your school or district?

_____

_____

_____

_____

_____

_____

_____

_____

_____

What would your next steps be, given what you have read so far?

_____

_____

_____

_____

_____

_____

_____

_____

_____

_____

_____

_____

_____

SECTION 2: CONNECTION TO HATTIE'S EFFECT SIZES IN RELATION TO THE CORE COMPONENTS OF CRT

Why Hattie's Effect Sizes?

In looking at what information about CRT would be helpful for educators, we went back to the question of what works best in education. That question also drove Hattie's comprehensive meta-analysis of areas that contribute to learning: the student, the home, the school, the classroom, the curricula, the teacher, and teaching and learning approaches (Hattie, 2018). Along with providing information on the relative effects of these influences on student achievement, Hattie also emphasized the importance of understanding and making visible the story of the underlying data. One of his most critical findings was how important it is to make teaching and learning visible. We agree and feel the same about making the teaching and learning of *behavior* visible. We've compared key components of CRT to influences Hattie identifies that impact student achievement. We feel these components are intrinsically linked to supporting a student's social emotional needs, and provide further evidence of the *why*; that is, implementation of these behavior initiatives is also critical to supporting a student's academic achievement. The following definition of key terms and description of how to interpret effect sizes will be a useful reference as you review the CRT table in this section.

HOW TO INTERPRET EFFECT SIZES

Hattie's work is based on achievement outcomes, while this book focuses on behaviors. We know that misbehavior can take away from students' achievement outcomes. A 1.0 standard deviation is typically associated with an increase in student achievement by two to three years. An effect size of 1.0 would mean that, on average, students receiving that treatment would exceed 84 percent of students not receiving the treatment. Hattie (2009) sets the benchmark of an effect size of $d = 0.4$ as the "hinge-point" where anything above it is labeled in the "zone of desired effects" as influences with the greatest impact on student learning. That doesn't mean that anything below 0.4 shouldn't be explored in greater detail. It just means that the influences aren't as great. Effects between $d = 0.15$ and $d = 0.40$ are typically what teachers could accomplish across an ordinary year of teaching. Ninety-five percent of everything we do has a positive influence on achievement, so setting the benchmark at anything above zero would be pointless. Furthermore, the zone between $d = 0.0$ and $d = 0.15$ is what students could achieve without schooling or by the simple process of maturation alone. Therefore, any effects below $d = 0.15$ are potentially harmful and should not be implemented. The remaining 5 percent of the factors have reverse effects, or decrease achievement. To put it simply, Hattie (2009) says that "students who do not achieve at least 0.40 improvement in a year are going backwards" (p. 250). Additionally, "It is a teacher who does not achieve an average of $d > 0.40$ per year that I do not want my children to experience" (p. 126).

Hattie presents his research through seven main contributors to learning (referred to as sources of influence): *the student, curricula, home, school, classroom, teacher, and teaching and learning approaches*. Hattie works through each of these sources of influence to evaluate which specific innovations and influences (factors) have the greatest impact on achievement. The factors are grouped by more specific "aspects" of each source of influence.

Visualize it like this:

1. **Teacher (*source of influence*)**
   a. Teacher attributes (*aspect*)
      i. Teacher estimates of student achievement (*factor*) (effect size [*d*] = 1.62)

2. **Student (*source of influence*)**
   a. Beliefs, attitudes, dispositions (*aspect*)
      i. Self-efficacy (*factor*) (*d* = 0.92)

The data in the table are listed from lowest effect size to highest. Remember, each source of influence is the broader category, and the subsets of each source are the aspects, which then group the various factors for each subset.

CRT: Connection to Hattie's Effect Sizes in Relation to the Core Components of This Behavior Initiative			
Source of Influence	**Aspect**	**Factor**	**Effect Size**
Home	Family dynamics	Corporal punishment in the home	−0.33
School	Other school effects	Suspending or expelling students	−0.2
Student	Beliefs, attitudes, dispositions	Morning vs. eveningness	0.12
Student	Motivation & mental state	Lack of stress	0.17
Home	Family structure	Divorced or remarried	0.23
Classroom	Classroom influences	Cognitive behavioral programs	0.29
Student	Beliefs, attitudes, dispositions	Mindfulness	0.29
School	Leadership	School climate	0.32
Student	Physical influences	Drugs	0.32
Classroom	Classroom influences	Decreasing disruptive behavior	0.34
Classroom	Classroom influences	Classroom management	0.35
Student	Beliefs, attitudes, dispositions	Self-concept	0.41
Student	Motivation & mental state	Motivation	0.42
Student	Motivation & mental state	Anxiety	0.42
Home	Family dynamics	Parental involvement	0.5
Home	Family resources	Socio-economic status	0.52
Home	Family dynamics	Home environment	0.52
Teacher	Teacher-student interactions	Teacher-student relationships	0.52
Teaching: student learning strategies	Meta-cognition/self-regulated learning	Self-regulation strategies	0.52
Student	Beliefs, attitudes, dispositions	Concentration, persistence, and engagement	0.56
Classroom	Classroom influences	Classroom behavior	0.62
Student	Beliefs, attitudes, dispositions	Self-efficacy	0.92
Teacher	Teacher attributes	Teacher estimates of student achievement	1.62

Source: Hattie, J. (2018, October). *Visible Learning^plus 250+ influences on student achievement.* Retrieved from https://us.corwin.com/sites/default/files/250_influences_10.1.2018.pdf. Retrieved February 4, 2019.

Educators tend to focus on the influences that have the most positive effects on student learning (those at the bottom of the preceding list), using that information to decide what to do more of. They don't generally look at the top of the list to identify what to do less of. Understanding this list from a strength and deficit lens allows educators to become more cognizant of the factors they influence directly, allowing them to target the effects these influences have on learning (e.g., by continuing, decreasing, or ending altogether certain practices) in order to create environments that reverse negative effects and increase positive effects on student success.

For example, teacher estimates of student achievement has an effect size of 1.62 on student achievement, which equates to two to three years of growth in student achievement in one year. Culturally responsive teaching requires teachers to have and hold high expectations for all students. Additionally, students' self-efficacy (their beliefs they can perform a given task) has an effect size of 0.92. Successful CRT necessitates that students' cultural connections be affirmed in a classroom environment that is managed with firm, consistent, and loving control by a teacher who facilitates learning while holding high expectations for his or her students.

We encourage you to use this information to help guide implementation of behavior initiatives.

Section 2: Questions to Consider

What connections can you make between the effect sizes of the common components of implementation of CRT and academic achievement?

_____

_____

_____

_____

_____

_____

_____

_____

_____

_____

_____

_____

_____

_____

_____

(Continued)

(Continued)

How will you use effect sizes to ask questions that will allow you to dig deeper to improve practice?

_____

_____

_____

_____

_____

_____

_____

_____

_____

_____

_____

How will you use this information with your colleagues to achieve the desired outcomes for students?

_____

_____

_____

_____

_____

_____

_____

_____

_____

_____

_____

_____

SECTION 3: SYNTHESIZED INDICATORS OF CRT IMPLEMENTATION SUCCESS AND CHALLENGES

To develop this synthesized list of indicators of CRT implementation success and challenges, we relied on our research and experiences as practitioners. Specifically, we used a combination of peer-reviewed research findings, practical application and experiences from the field, and expert testimonials as our reference to identify common implementation success trends and challenge trends. We wanted to provide this information as you consider implementation of this behavior initiative.

CRT: Synthesized Indicators of Implementation Success and Challenges	
Implementation Success Trends	**Implementation Challenge Trends**
Belief in and communication of high expectations	Belief that CRT is a new type of teaching only relevant to low-income, urban students of color
Proper training provided for implementation	
Embedding CRT in every classroom	Belief that CRT requires teachers to master the details of every culture represented from the students in their classrooms
Focus on building students' resilience and mindset	
Educators who have an authentic interest in cultural backgrounds and language of the children and families they serve	Belief that only teachers of color are capable of demonstrating the essential elements of CRT in schools with diverse student populations
Focus on the cognitive development of underserved students	Belief that CRT reinforces stereotypes about children of color because this pedagogy categorizes and labels children based on their race and ethnicity
Student-centered instruction	
Teachers who learn about and respect their students' cultural backgrounds; culture, language, and racial identity	Belief that CRT is a "bag of tricks" that diminishes the complexity of teaching some students of color
Teachers who adapt their teaching methods for various learning styles	Belief that it's just "good teaching"
Teachers and families are effective partners	Belief that children from all cultures learn the same
Collaborative teaching	Lack of adequate materials

Section 3: Question to Consider

To what extent will you use the synthesized indicators of implementation success and challenges to prevent obstacles during implementation?

_____

_____

_____

_____

_____

_____

_____

_____

SECTION 4: CRT BEST-PRACTICE RESOURCE INVENTORY

To develop this best-practice resource inventory for CRT implementation, we again used as our reference points a combination of research and best practices in the field based on our experiences. For example, we included effective resources based on (1) peer-reviewed research findings and (2) data from schools and districts implementing CRT with effective outcomes for students. This information could be used as a starting point for looking into best-practice resources to assist with your implementation of CRT. *Note:* We understand that other resources are available. What is provided here is what we found based on the aforementioned criteria for this best-practice resource inventory.

CRT: Best-Practice Resource Inventory		
Resource	Description *Note:* Some of the descriptions in this column are quoted directly from the listed resources.	References
"A Framework for Culturally Responsive Teaching" (outlines the intrinsic motivational framework as a model of culturally responsive teaching)	The framework names four motivational conditions that the teacher and students continuously create or enhance. They are: 1. Establishing inclusion—creating a learning atmosphere in which students and teachers feel respected by and connected to one another. 2. Developing attitude—creating a favorable disposition toward the learning experience through personal relevance and choice. 3. Enhancing meaning—creating challenging, thoughtful learning experiences that include student perspectives and values. 4. Engendering competence—creating an understanding that students are effective in learning something they value.	Wlodkowski and Ginsberg (1995)
Culturally Responsive Teaching: Theory, Research, and Practice, 2nd edition	The text includes: • Expanded coverage of student ethnic groups: African and Latino Americans as well as Asian and Native Americans. • A new section on standards and diversity. • New examples of culturally diverse curriculum content. • More examples of programs and techniques that exemplify culturally responsive teaching. • An emphasis on positive, action-driven possibilities in student–teacher relationships. • New material on culturally diverse communication, addressing common myths about language diversity and the effects of "English Plus" instruction.	Gay (2010)
"As Diversity Grows, So Must We"	Outlines the five phases of CRT transformative work: (1) building trust, (2) engaging personal culture, (3) confronting issues of social dominance and social justice, (4) transforming instructional practices, and (5) engaging the entire school community.	Howard (2007)

CRT: Best-Practice Resource Inventory

Resource	Description *Note:* Some of the descriptions in this column are quoted directly from the listed resources.	References
"But That's Just Good Teaching! The Case for Culturally Relevant Pedagogy"	This journal article is written by an expert in culturally relevant pedagogy. This short article provides a good overview of the research and practices related to CRT.	Ladson-Billings (1995a)
"Culturally Responsive Teaching"	This paper features an innovation configuration (IC) matrix that can guide teacher preparation professionals in the development of appropriate culturally responsive teaching (CRT) content.	Aceves and Orosco (2014)
"Toward a Theory of Culturally Relevant Pedagogy"	This article attempts to challenge notions about the intersection of culture and teaching that rely solely on microanalytic or macroanalytic perspectives. Rather, the article attempts to build on the work done in both of these areas and proposes a culturally relevant theory of education. By raising questions about the location of the researcher in pedagogical research, the article attempts to explicate the theoretical framework of the author in the nexus of collaborative and reflexive research. The pedagogical practices of eight exemplary teachers of African-American students serve as the investigative "site." Their practices and reflections on those practices provide a way to define and recognize culturally relevant pedagogy.	Ladson-Billings (1995b)
"Toward a Conceptual Framework of Culturally Relevant Pedagogy"	Provides an overview of theoretical research	Brown-Jeffy & Cooper (2011)
The Dreamkeepers: Successful Teachers of African-American Students, 2nd edition	In the second edition of her critically acclaimed book *The Dreamkeepers*, Gloria Ladson-Billings revisits the eight teachers who were profiled in the first edition and introduces us to new teachers who are current exemplars of good teaching. She shows that culturally relevant teaching is not a matter of race, gender, or teaching style. What matters most is a teacher's efforts to work with the unique strengths a child brings to the classroom. A brilliant mixture of scholarship and storytelling, *The Dreamkeepers* challenges us to envision intellectually rigorous and culturally relevant classrooms that have the power to improve the lives of not just African American students, but all children. This new edition also includes questions for reflection.	Ladson-Billings (1994)
Culturally Responsive Teaching and the Brain: Promoting Authentic Engagement and Rigor Among Culturally and Linguistically Diverse Students	A bold, brain-based teaching approach to culturally responsive instruction To close the achievement gap, diverse classrooms need a proven framework for optimizing student engagement. Culturally responsive instruction has shown promise, but many teachers have struggled with its implementation—until now. In this book, Zaretta Hammond draws on cutting-edge neuroscience research to offer an innovative approach for designing and implementing brain-compatible culturally responsive instruction.	Hammond (2014); for companion study guide, see https://crtandthebrain.com/

Culturally Responsive Teaching

(Continued)

CRT: Best-Practice Resource Inventory (Continued)		
Resource	Description *Note:* Some of the descriptions in this column are quoted directly from the listed resources.	References
	The book includes: • Information on how one's culture programs the brain to process data and affects learning relationships • Ten "key moves" to build students' learner operating systems and prepare them to become independent learners • Prompts for action and valuable self-reflection	
Teaching Tolerance Website	Teaching Tolerance provides free resources to educators—teachers, administrators, counsellors and other practitioners—who work with children from kindergarten through high school. Educators use our materials to supplement the curriculum, to inform their practices, and to create civil and inclusive school communities where children are respected, valued and welcome participants.	https://www.tolerance.org/

Section 4: Questions to Consider

What resources do you think would help with your implementation of this behavior initiative?

_____

_____

_____

_____

_____

_____

_____

_____

_____

_____

_____

Name one resource listed that you will investigate further and why.

_____

_____

_____

_____

_____

_____

_____

_____

_____

_____

_____

_____

_____

_____

_____

_____

_____

_____

_____

_____

_____

_____

TRAUMA-INFORMED PRACTICES

IN THIS CHAPTER you will find information on trauma-informed practices (TIPs) divided into four sections, each followed by questions to consider to help you evaluate this behavior initiative and guide meaningful discussions around possible implementation in your school or district.

Section 1: The *What*—Trauma-Informed Practices (TIPs)

Section 2: Connection to Hattie's Effect Sizes in Relation to the Core Components of TIPs

Section 3: Synthesized Indicators of TIPs Implementation Success and Challenges

Section 4: TIPs Best-Practice Resource Inventory

SECTION 1: THE *WHAT*— TRAUMA-INFORMED PRACTICES (TIPs)

Behavior is a form of communication. Many of our students come to school speaking a different behavior language: some are loud, while others scream quietly. Research tells us that when educators are trauma-informed, students will learn how to express their emotions in appropriate ways. And just like their counterparts, English language learners, learning a new behavior language takes time, consistent positive reinforcement and environments that create a sense of belonging and emotional safety.

—Victoria E. Romero
Coauthor, *Building Resilience in Students Impacted by Adverse Childhood Experiences: A Whole Staff Approach*

Simply put, trauma-informed practices (TIPs) is a structure designed to help educators provide a safe, informed, and understanding learning environment for students or staff impacted by direct or secondary trauma. However, there are some noteworthy variations in common TIPs definitions and styles of implementation. Even given the variations, the intended outcomes for TIPs implementation are similar.

Each chapter in Part II is divided into four sections that end with questions to help guide discussions with your teacher or leadership teams around each behavior initiative. As you navigate through this chapter, remember to use the Behavior Initiatives K-W-L strategy to help organize your learnings around TIPs implementation, beginning with the purpose for implementing TIPs and common definitions (i.e., the *what*).

Purpose for TIPs

- Reduce traumatic stress of students and adults
- Create a welcoming and safe environment
- Learn how to prevent retraumatization
- Teach emotional regulation skills
- Reduce depression symptoms in students
- Reduce suspensions and expulsions
- Increase student achievement
- Improve school culture

- Help students who have been impacted by family/home violence or other traumatic events
- Help students feel safe and supported to learn
- Help staff develop awareness
- Create a culture of trauma sensitivity
- Develop a sense of family at the school
- Provide opportunities for relationship building

Variations of TIPs

Based on our experiences helping schools implement behavior initiatives and through our research findings, we have noticed that there are multiple definitions or variations of the six behavior initiatives outlined in this book. That can be overwhelming while you are trying to decide which behavior initiative is best for your school or district, so we outline three common definitions for each of the six behavior initiatives identified in this book, based on repeated mentions of them through the research and in the field. *Note:* If a definition you prefer is not cited in this section, it does not mean it is not a worthy definition to use. We just want to provide a few examples of common definitions to help educators better understand each behavior initiative.

We strongly believe that school or district staff need to understand the *what* definition and the rest of the information in each of these chapters in order to make informed decisions about implementation.

THREE COMMON TIPs DEFINITIONS

Common Definition 1: Based on the Substance Abuse and Mental Health Services Administration (SAMHSA) definition of a trauma-informed approach, trauma-informed practice is "a program, organization, or system" that

- Realizes the widespread impact of trauma and understands potential paths for recovery;

- Recognizes the signs and symptoms of trauma in clients, families, staff, and others involved with the system;

- Responds by fully integrating knowledge about trauma into policies, procedures, and practices; and

- Seeks to actively resist re-traumatization.

A trauma-informed approach reflects adherence to six key principles rather than a prescribed set of practices or procedures. These principles may be generalizable across multiple types of settings, although terminology and application may be setting- or sector-specific:

1. Safety

2. Trustworthiness and transparency

3. Peer support

4. Collaboration and mutuality

5. Empowerment, voice, and choice

6. Cultural, historical, and gender issues

"A trauma-informed approach can be implemented in any type of service setting or organization and is distinct from trauma-specific interventions or treatments that are designed specifically to address the consequences of trauma and to facilitate healing" (SAMHSA, n.d.).

Common Definition 2: Trauma-informed practice is used when "the adults in the school community are prepared to recognize and respond to those who have been impacted by traumatic stress. Those adults include administrators, teachers, staff, parents, and law enforcement. In addition, students are provided with clear expectations and communication strategies to guide them through stressful situations. The goal is to not only provide tools to cope with extreme situations but to create an underlying culture of respect and support" (Treatment and Services Adaptation Center, n.d.).

Common Definition 3: Trauma-informed practice is defined according to the Flexible Framework ("Six Elements of School Operations Involved in Creating a Trauma-Sensitive School"). The Flexible Framework "enables schools and districts—in collaboration with families, local community organizations, and outside providers—to maintain a whole school focus as they create trauma sensitive schools. The Framework is organized according to six core operational functions of schools, each of which is critical to any effort that seeks to make school-wide changes" (Trauma and Learning Policy Initiative, n.d.):

1. Leadership

2. Professional Development

3. Access to Resources and Services

4. Academic and Nonacademic Strategies

5. Policies and Protocols

6. Collaboration with Families

In Chapter 1 of this book, we shared a snapshot of a TIPs school as a reference. We also want to provide a before-and-after story to help reinforce the beliefs and behaviors necessary for implementing TIPs in your school or district.

A BEFORE-AND-AFTER TIPs STORY

Before TIPs . . . student trauma was not considered as a reason for students not behaving or accessing their education. Teachers at this school claimed they did not go to school to be social workers and that they needed more mental health resources available at their school. They complained that they could not teach all the other students due to these extreme behaviors that were taking over their classroom instruction. More and more students began to demonstrate symptoms of burnout at the school. Teacher absences increased by double digits from the prior year. Teachers felt like administrators were doing nothing about discipline or providing supports for these students, and they did not feel equipped to respond themselves.

After TIPs . . . teachers began to learn about the impact of trauma and the different ways students can behave as a result. Teachers worked with the administration team to create safe zones within and outside their classroom settings where students could take a break and calm their emotions with their learned skills instead of kicking them out and insisting they be suspended. Students felt safe in their classrooms and at school and knew they could go to an adult who cared about them if needed. In addition, support service providers worked closely with teachers to put safeguards and proper interventions in place for students in crisis.

Section 1: Questions to Consider

What are the intended outcomes of your school's or district's TIPs initiative?

_____

_____

_____

_____

_____

_____

_____

_____

_____

_____

How does your school or district define TIPs?

_____

_____

_____

_____

_____

_____

What is currently in place at your school or district?

_____

_____

_____

_____

_____

_____

What would your next steps be, given what you have read so far?

_____

_____

_____

_____

_____

_____

_____

Trauma-Informed Practices

SECTION 2: CONNECTION TO HATTIE'S EFFECT SIZES IN RELATION TO THE CORE COMPONENTS OF TIPs

Why Hattie's Effect Sizes?

In looking at what information about TIPs would be helpful for educators, we went back to the question of what works best in education. That question also drove Hattie's comprehensive meta-analysis of areas that contribute to learning: the student, the home, the school, the classroom, the curricula, the teacher, and teaching and learning approaches (Hattie, 2018). Along with providing information on the relative effects of these influences on student achievement, Hattie also emphasized the importance of understanding and making visible the story of the underlying data. One of his most critical findings was how important it is to make teaching and learning visible. We agree and feel the same about making the teaching and learning of *behavior* visible. We've compared key components of TIPs to influences Hattie identifies that impact student achievement. We feel these components are intrinsically linked to supporting a student's social emotional needs, and provide further evidence of the *why*; that is, implementation of these behavior initiatives is also critical to supporting a student's academic achievement. The following definition of key terms and description of how to interpret effect sizes will be a useful reference as you review the TIPs table in this section.

HOW TO INTERPRET EFFECT SIZES

Hattie's work is based on achievement outcomes, while this book focuses on behaviors. We know that misbehavior can take away from students' achievement outcomes. A 1.0 standard deviation is typically associated with an increase in student achievement by two to three years. An effect size of 1.0 would mean that, on average, students receiving that treatment would exceed 84 percent of students not receiving the treatment. Hattie (2009) sets the benchmark of an effect size of $d = 0.4$ as the "hinge-point" where anything above it is labeled in the "zone of desired effects" as influences with the greatest impact on student learning. That doesn't mean that anything below 0.4 shouldn't be explored in greater detail. It just means that the influences aren't as great. Effects between $d = 0.15$ and $d = 0.40$ are typically what teachers could accomplish across an ordinary year of teaching. Ninety-five percent of everything we do has a positive influence on achievement, so setting the benchmark at anything above zero would be pointless. Furthermore, the zone between $d = 0.0$ and $d = 0.15$ is what students could achieve without schooling or by the simple process of maturation alone. Therefore, any effects below $d = 0.15$ are potentially harmful and should not be implemented. The remaining 5 percent of the factors have reverse effects, or decrease achievement. To put it simply, Hattie (2009) says that "students who do not achieve at least 0.40 improvement in a year are going backwards" (p. 250). Additionally, "It is a teacher who does not achieve an average of $d > 0.40$ per year that I do not want my children to experience" (p. 126).

Hattie presents his research through seven main contributors to learning (referred to as sources of influence): *the student, curricula, home, school, classroom, teacher, and teaching and learning approaches*. Hattie works through each of these sources of influence to evaluate which specific innovations and influences (factors) have the greatest impact on achievement. The factors are grouped by more specific "aspects" of each source of influence.

Visualize it like this:

1. **Teaching: student learning strategies (*source of influence*)**
   a. Metacognition/self-regulated learning (*aspect*)
      i. Self-regulation strategies (*factor*) (effect size [*d*] = 0.52)

2. **Home (*source of influence*)**
   a. Home environment (*aspect*)
      i. Parental military deployment (*factor*) ($d = -0.16$)

The data in the table are listed from lowest effect size to highest. Remember, each source of influence is the broader category, and the subsets of each source are the aspects, which then group the various factors for each subset.

TIPs: Connection to Hattie's Effect Sizes in Relation to the Core Components of This Behavior Initiative			
Source of Influence	**Aspect**	**Factor**	**Effect Size**
Student	Physical influences	ADHD	−0.9
Student	Motivation & mental state	Depression	−0.36
Home	Family dynamics	Corporal punishment in the home	−0.33
School	Other school effects	Suspending or expelling students	−0.2
Home	Home environment	Parental military deployment	−0.16
Student	Beliefs, attitudes, dispositions	Morning vs. eveningness	0.12
Student	Motivation & mental state	Lack of stress	0.17
Home	Family structure	Divorced or remarried	0.23
Classroom	Classroom influences	Cognitive behavioral programs	0.29
Student	Beliefs, attitudes, dispositions	Mindfulness	0.29
School	Leadership	School climate	0.32
Student	Physical influences	Drugs	0.32
Classroom	Classroom influences	Decreasing disruptive behavior	0.34
Classroom	Classroom influences	Classroom management	0.35
Student	Beliefs, attitudes, dispositions	Self-concept	0.41
Student	Motivation & mental state	Motivation	0.42
Student	Motivation & mental state	Anxiety	0.42
Home	Family dynamics	Parental involvement	0.5
Home	Family resources	Socio-economic status	0.52
Home	Family dynamics	Home environment	0.52
Teacher	Teacher-student interactions	Teacher-student relationships	0.52
Teaching: student learning strategies	Metacognition/self-regulated learning	Self-regulation strategies	0.52
Student	Beliefs, attitudes, dispositions	Concentration, persistence, and engagement	0.56
Classroom	Classroom influences	Classroom behavioral	0.62
Student	Beliefs, attitudes, dispositions	Self-efficacy	0.92
Teacher	Teacher attributes	Teacher estimates of student achievement	1.62

Source: Hattie, J. (2018, October). *Visible Learning^plus 250+ influences on student achievement.* Retrieved from https://us.corwin.com/sites/default/files/250_influences_10.1.2018.pdf. Retrieved February 4, 2019.

Trauma-Informed Practices

Educators tend to focus on the influences that have the most positive effects on student learning (those at the bottom of the preceding list), using that information to decide what to do more of. They don't generally look at the top of the list to identify what to do less of. Understanding this list from a strength and deficit lens allows educators to become more cognizant of the factors they influence directly, allowing them to target the effects these influences have on learning (e.g., by continuing, decreasing, or ending altogether certain practices) in order to create environments that reverse negative effects and increase positive effects on student success.

For example, parental military deployment has an effect size of −0.16 on student achievement, which equates to a negative (or reverse) effect on learning. Knowing the negative effect and stress that parental military deployment has on a student's ability to focus on learning, the adults in the school community are prepared to recognize and respond to those who have been impacted by traumatic stress and can effectively guide them through stressful situations.

We encourage you to use this information to help guide implementation of behavior initiatives.

Section 2: Questions to Consider

What connections can you make between the effect sizes of the common components of implementation of TIPs and academic achievement?

_____

_____

_____

_____

_____

_____

_____

_____

_____

_____

_____

_____

_____

How will you use effect sizes to ask questions that will allow you to dig deeper to improve practice?

_____

_____

_____

_____

_____

_____

_____

_____

_____

How will you use this information with your colleagues to achieve the desired outcomes for students?

_____

_____

_____

_____

_____

_____

_____

_____

_____

Trauma-Informed Practices

SECTION 3: SYNTHESIZED INDICATORS OF TIPs IMPLEMENTATION SUCCESS AND CHALLENGES

To develop this synthesized list of indicators of TIPs implementation success and challenges, we relied on our research and experiences as practitioners. Specifically, we used a combination of peer-reviewed research findings, practical application and experiences from the field, and expert testimonials as our reference to identify common implementation success trends and challenge trends. We wanted to provide this information as you consider implementation of this behavior initiative.

TIPs: Synthesized Indicators of Implementation Success and Challenges	
Implementation Success Trends	**Implementation Challenge Trends**
The expectation of the way the adults interact in front of the children	Staff not trained adequately
Build connection with students	Not embedded in laws or policies
Promote resiliency	Limited resources allocated for implementation
Recognize the signs and symptoms of trauma in students, family, and staff	Not implemented as a schoolwide approach
Establish predictable and coherent school and classroom environments	Not enough qualified supports on campus
Integrate knowledge about trauma into policies, procedures, and practices	Use of exclusionary practices
Resist retraumatization of students and staff and foster resiliency	No safe space or supports available
Link with mental health professionals, academic instruction for traumatized students, and other strategies to help traumatized students be successful in all aspects of the school day	Not teaching through a trauma-informed lens
	Triggering students
	Not a timely response
	Lack of communication with all stakeholders
Ongoing professional development activities for all staff	No clear roles and responsibilities for implementation
All staff receive training and establish communication channels	Surface-level implementation
Full-time trauma-informed school or district coordinator or lead identified to help align existing systems, structures, and programs, and to plan	
Provide ongoing support and resources for staff, and develop student and family engagement plans	
Review policies, procedures, programs, and services with community service partners to be more trauma-informed	

Section 3: Question to Consider

To what extent will you use the synthesized indicators of implementation success and challenges to prevent obstacles during implementation?

_____

_____

_____

_____

_____

_____

_____

_____

_____

_____

_____

_____

_____

_____

_____

_____

_____

_____

_____

_____

_____

SECTION 4: TIPs BEST-PRACTICE RESOURCE INVENTORY

To develop this best-practice resource inventory for TIPs implementation, we again used as our reference points a combination of research and best practices in the field based on our experiences. For example, we included effective resources based on (1) peer-reviewed research findings and (2) data from schools and districts implementing TIPs with effective outcomes for students. This information could be used as a starting point for looking into best-practice resources to assist with your implementation of TIPs. *Note:* We understand that other resources are available. What is provided here is what we found based on the aforementioned criteria for this best-practice resource inventory.

TIPs: Best-Practice Resource Inventory		
Resource	Description *Note:* Some of the descriptions in this column are quoted directly from the listed resources.	References
Child Trauma Toolkit for Educators	A Cognitive Behavioral Intervention for Trauma in Schools program shown to reduce traumatic stress and depressions symptoms and to increase the grade point average of traumatized students. Components: (a) Trauma Facts for Educators, (b) Understanding Child Traumatic Stress: A Guide for Parents, (c) Psychological and Behavioral Impact of Trauma: Elementary School Students, (d) Psychological and Behavioral Impact of Trauma: Middle School Students, (e) Psychological and Behavioral Impact of Trauma: High School Students, (f) Self Care for Educators, (g) Suggestions for Educators, (h) Brief Information on Childhood Traumatic Grief, (i) Brief Information on Childhood Traumatic Grief for School Personnel, and (j) Students and Trauma DVD.	http://www.nctsn.org
The Sanctuary Model	Sanctuary Model is not a specific intervention, but a full system approach focused on creating an organizational culture designed to help injured clients recover from the damaging effects of interpersonal trauma. The aims of the Sanctuary Model are to guide an organization in the development of a culture with seven dominant characteristics, all of which serve goals that simultaneously create a sound treatment environment, while counteracting the impact of chronic and unrelenting stress: 1. **Culture of Nonviolence**—building and modeling safety skills and a commitment to higher goals 2. **Culture of Emotional Intelligence**—teaching and modeling emotional management skills and the integration of thoughts and feelings 3. **Culture of Social Learning**—building and modeling cognitive skills in an environment that promotes conflict resolution and transformation 4. **Culture of Shared Governance**—creating and modeling civic skills of self-control, self-discipline, and administration of healthy authority 5. **Culture of Open Communication**—overcoming barriers to healthy communication, reducing acting-out, enhancing self-protective and self-correcting skills, teaching healthy boundaries	http://www.sanctuaryweb.com/schools.php

TIPs: Best-Practice Resource Inventory		
Resource	Description *Note:* Some of the descriptions in this column are quoted directly from the listed resources.	References
	6. **Culture of Social Responsibility**—rebuilding social connection skills, establishing healthy attachment relationships 7. **Culture of Growth and Change**—working through loss; restoring hope, meaning, purpose.	
The Adverse Childhood Experiences (ACE) Study	The researchers asked people to place themselves into eight categories of adverse childhood experiences by answering the following questions. Before the age of eighteen: • Were you physically or psychologically abused by a parent? • Did anyone sexually abuse you? • Were you emotionally or physically neglected? • Was anyone in your household violent against your mother? • Was anyone in the household mentally ill or abused drugs and/or alcohol? • Was there anyone in the household who was imprisoned? • Were your parents divorced or separated? The number of categories (not the number of occurrences) of these adverse childhood experiences was then compared to measures of adult risk behavior, health status, and disease. The number of categories—not events—that the person admitted to then became their ACE score which essentially represents their "trauma dose" as children.	http://www.cdc.gov/nccdphp/ace/ ACEs Overview: https://www.samhsa.gov/capt/practicingeffective-prevention/prevention behavioral-health/adverse-childhood experiences CDC-Kaiser ACE Study: https://www.cdc.gov/violenceprevention/childabuseandneglect/acestudy/aboutace.html
S.E.L.F.: A Trauma-Informed Implementation Tool	S.E.L.F. is the implementation tool that is a fundamental component of the Sanctuary Model, an acronym that stands for Safety, Emotional management, Loss, and Future. S.E.L.F. is a conceptual tool (originally called S.A.G.E.) . . . that guides assessment, treatment planning, individual and team discussion, and the psychoeducational group work. S.E.L.F. is not a staged treatment model, but rather a non-linear method for addressing, in simple words, very complex challenges. The four concepts: Safety, Emotions, Loss, and Future represent the four fundamental domains of disruption that can occur in a person's life. Within these four domains, any problem can be categorized. Naming and categorization are the first steps in making a problem manageable. Victims of overwhelming life experiences have difficulty staying safe, find emotions difficult to manage, have suffered many losses, and have difficulty envisioning a future. As a result, they are frequently in danger, lose emotional control, or are so numb that they cannot access their emotions, have many signs of unresolved loss, and are stuck in time, haunted by the past, and unable to move into a better future.	Bloom and Sreedhar (2008); http://www.sanctuaryweb.com

(Continued)

TIPs: Best-Practice Resource Inventory (Continued)		
Resource	**Description** *Note:* Some of the descriptions in this column are quoted directly from the listed resources.	**References**
Psychological First Aid—Listen, Protect, Connect	Psychological first aid (PFA) began as a tool to help first responders cope with victims experiencing trauma on the scene. There are several models of PFA, but Psychological First Aid—Listen, Protect, Connect (PFA—LPC) was developed in response to a series of school shootings in the 1990s. The five-step crisis response strategy was intended to guide teachers and staff members in helping traumatized students deal with the aftermath of senseless violence. PFA—LPC helps educational staff support students through the process of recovery, especially when students encounter traumatic reminders of being in danger or of experiencing loss or trauma. The main goals of PFA—LPC are: • To stabilize the emotions and behaviors of students • To return students to an improved mental and emotional state after a crisis or disaster ready to attend school and re-engage in learning While targeted at trauma-exposed students, PFA—LPC is beneficial to anyone who has experienced trauma. The strategy focuses on what a person needs in the moment to get through a difficult time.	http://traumaaware schools.org/pfa
UCSF's HEARTS program—Healthy Environments and Response to Trauma in Schools (HEARTS)	HEARTS is a whole-school, prevention and intervention approach that utilizes a multi-tiered system of supports (MTSS) framework to address trauma and chronic stress at the student level, staff level, and school organizational level. . . . Some of the supports provided by UCSF HEARTS across the three tiers when the full, site-based program is implemented: We aim to increase instructional time and decrease time spent on disciplinary actions. Specifically, the goals of HEARTS include: • Increasing student wellness, engagement, and success in school • Building staff and school system capacities to support trauma-impacted students by increasing knowledge and practice of trauma-informed classroom and school-wide strategies • Promoting staff wellness through addressing burnout and secondary traumatic stress • Interrupting the school to prison pipeline through the reduction of racial disparities in disciplinary office referrals, suspensions, and expulsions	http://hearts.ucsf.edu/ program-overview
Mindful Schools	Looking to take courses or find a like-minded community focused on creating trauma-sensitive schools? In need of resources including articles, multimedia, or a certified instructor directory? Founded in 2007, Mindful Schools started out as a program of a single school in Oakland, CA, and expanded into a non-profit training organization that offers online and in-person courses, content, and a network of mindful educators spanning all 50 U.S. states and 100+ countries.	https://www.mind fulschools.org/

TIPs: Best-Practice Resource Inventory		
Resource	Description *Note:* Some of the descriptions in this column are quoted directly from the listed resources.	References
Narrative Counseling in Schools: Powerful & Brief, 2nd edition	Help students shed negative labels and develop healthy behaviors! This updated edition will assist students in narrating stories that "redescribe" who they are and who they can be. "Another way to say all this is that a narrative perspective locates problems in the cultural landscape, which implies the counselors who are seeking to help need to consider their own and the client's cultural position" (p. 3).	Winslade and Monk (2007)
Changing Minds	Celebrate, Comfort, Collaborate, Listen, Inspire	https://changingmindsnow.org/healing
Youth WRAP: Wellness Recovery Action Plan, by Mary Ellen Copeland	This WRAP presents a system that helps young people make their lives more the way they want them to be, to choose and enjoy more of the things they want to do, and to get through the hard times that can come with finishing school, finding work, and moving into new situations for home, school, and family. When you make your WRAP, you choose what you will do every day, and if difficult things come up, you plan what your responses will be to keep yourself safe and in control of your life. You choose if you want to make a WRAP and what will go in your plan. Change it when you want to. It's yours! This book will help you: • Do what you want with your life • Discover your own simple, safe Wellness Tools • Develop a daily plan to help you stay as well as possible • Identify upsetting events or circumstances and develop action plans for responding to them • Create a strategy to gain support and stay in control of your wellness during and after a crisis	http://www.mentalhealthrecovery.com/store/youth-wrap_moreinfo.html
Compassionate Schools	*The Heart of Learning: Compassion, Resiliency, and Academic Success* is a handbook for teachers written and compiled by OSPI and Western Washington University staff. It contains valuable information that will be helpful to you on a daily basis as you work with students whose learning has been adversely impacted by trauma in their lives. **Chapter 1:** Trauma, Compassion, and Resiliency: Background and Definitions **Chapter 2:** Self-Care: An Ethical Obligation for Those Who Care **Chapter 3:** Instructional Principles, Curricular Domains and Specific Strategies for Compassionate Classrooms **Chapter 4:** Building Compassionate School-Community Partnerships That Work **Chapter 5:** Examples of Compassion, Resiliency, and Academic Success Direct From the Field **Chapter 6:** Resources	http://www.k12.wa.us/CompassionateSchools/HeartofLearning.aspx

Trauma-Informed Practices

(Continued)

TIPs: Best-Practice Resource Inventory (Continued)		
Resource	**Description** *Note:* **Some of the descriptions in this column are quoted directly from the listed resources.**	**References**
Making SPACE for Learning: Trauma-Informed Practice in Schools	Making SPACE for Learning is a resource guide to assist schools to unlock the potential of traumatized children and young people to grow and develop at school. This publication 1) explains how trauma can impact child development and functioning, including learning; 2) promotes five principles for trauma-informed schools using the acronym SPACE (Staged, Predictable, Adaptive, Connected, and Enabled); and 3) lists many concrete, specific trauma-sensitive strategies schools can implement.	https://professionals .childhood.org.au/ resources/
Substance Abuse and Mental Health Services Administration (SAMHSA) Trauma-Informed Approach and Trauma-Specific Interventions	A trauma-informed approach reflects adherence to six key principles rather than a prescribed set of practices or procedures. These principles may be generalizable across multiple types of settings, although terminology and application may be setting- or sector-specific: 1. Safety 2. Trustworthiness and transparency 3. Peer support 4. Collaboration and mutuality 5. Empowerment, voice and choice 6. Cultural, historical, and gender issues From SAMHSA's perspective, it is critical to promote the linkage to recovery and resilience for those individuals and families impacted by trauma. Consistent with SAMHSA's definition of recovery, services and supports that are trauma-informed build on the best evidence available and consumer and family engagement, empowerment, and collaboration.	https://www.samhsa .gov/nctic/trauma -interventions
Treating Trauma and Traumatic Grief in Children and Adolescents, 2nd edition	Trauma-Focused Cognitive Behavioral Therapy (TF-CBT) has the strongest research evidence of any treatment program for children who have experienced trauma. Through individual sessions with the child and joint sessions between the parent and child, TF-CBT interventions can be remembered using the "PRACTICE" acronym: psychoeducation and parenting skills, relaxation skills, affect regulation skills, cognitive coping and processing skills, trauma narrative, in vivo exposure, conjoint parent-child sessions, and enhancing safety. **Description:** A structured parent and child intervention which aims to teach youth skills on how to manage stress triggered by traumatic memories. **Intervention components:** Intervention is divided into three phases: (1) coping skills, (2) trauma narrative, and (3) parent/child sessions to share narrative and develop safety plan. **Structure:** Program consists of 8–20 individual sessions with the child or non-offending caregiver along with joint sessions.	Cohen, McCabe, Michelli, and Pickeral (2016)

TIPs: Best-Practice Resource Inventory		
Resource	Description *Note:* Some of the descriptions in this column are quoted directly from the listed resources.	References
Cognitive Behavioral Intervention for Trauma in Schools (CBITS)	Cognitive Behavioral Intervention for Trauma in Schools (CBITS) is an evidence-supported intervention designed for use in schools with children who have experienced trauma. It includes group and individual sessions, as well as psychoeducational sessions for parents and training for teachers. **Description:** School-based group and individual intervention whose goals are threefold: (1) reduce symptoms related to trauma exposure, (2) teach and build skills to manage trauma-related stress, and (3) build caregiver and peer support. **Intervention components:** Intervention incorporates six essential cognitive behavioral elements: (1) psychoeducation on how trauma affects students, (2) relaxation strategies, (3) cognitive restructuring, (4) graduated in vivo exposure, (5) trauma exposure, and (6) social problem solving. **Structure:** The program consists of 10 group sessions for children, 1–3 individual sessions for children, 2 group educational sessions for parents, and 1 educational session for teachers. **Population:** students 5th through 12th grade. CBITS has been adapted for Spanish-speaking populations, low-literacy groups, and children in foster care. CBITS has also been implemented in mental health clinics.	Jaycox, Langley, and Hoover (2018)
Support for Students Exposed to Trauma (SSET)	CBITS has also been modified to be delivered by teachers and school counselors to middle school students. The modified program is called Support for Students Exposed to Trauma (SSET). The SSET was designed for implementation by teachers and school counselors, and the program manual including lesson plans is available for download. When trained clinicians are not available at a school to provide trauma-specific treatment, school staff should consider implementing programs such as SSET designed for non-clinicians or refer students to outside interventions to promote healing from past traumas.	Jaycox, Langley, and Dean (2009)
Grief and Trauma Intervention (GTI) for Children	This intervention combines techniques from cognitive behavioral therapy (CBT) and narrative therapy to address children's symptoms of trauma and loss. The three main goals of the intervention are to help children (1) learn more about grief and traumatic reactions (education), (2) express their thoughts and feelings about what happened (trauma narrative), and (3) reduce symptoms of posttraumatic stress, depression, and traumatic grief. Intervention components: GTI is comprised of three overlapping phases: (1) resilience and safety (Sessions 1–5), (2) restorative retelling (Sessions 6–9), and (3) reconnecting (Sessions 8–10). **Structure:** The program consists of 10 sessions and a parent meeting. It can be conducted in a group or individual format. When conducted with groups, each child also receives an individual "pull out" session. **Population:** children ages 7–12	Jaycox, Langley, and Hoover (2018)

Trauma-Informed Practices

(Continued)

TIPs: Best-Practice Resource Inventory (Continued)		
Resource	**Description** *Note:* **Some of the descriptions in this column are quoted directly from the listed resources.**	**References**
Risking Connections	Risking Connections is a trauma-informed model that emphasizes the importance of "RICH" relationships (i.e., relationships marked by respect, information sharing, connection, and hope) and self-care for service providers working with individuals who have experienced trauma.	http://www.risking connection.com/
Trauma-Informed Organizational Self-Assessment	This self-assessment tool was designed for use by homeless services providers but could be adapted and used in the school setting to evaluate and improve practices to better support students who have experienced trauma.	National Council for Behavioral Health, thenationalcouncil.org
Multimodal Trauma Treatment (MMTT); also known as Trauma-Focused Coping in Schools	**Description:** School-based group intervention that is skills-oriented and a peer-mediating group treatment for youth exposed to single-incident trauma. **Intervention components:** Intervention components are delivered per session as follows: (1) psycho education, (2) anxiety management, (3–4) anxiety management and cognitive training, (5a, 5b) anger coping and grief management, (6) individual pull out session for narrative exposure, (7) developing stimulus hierarchy, (8–10) group narrative exposure, (11) worst moment cognitive and affective processing, (12, 13) relapse prevention, and (14) graduation. **Structure:** The program is delivered as a 14-session group therapy during one class period per week. Additionally, there is one individual pull out session midway through the intervention to work on the narrative exposure. **Population:** children and adolescents ages 9–18 or grades 4 through 12.	Chafouleas, Johnson, Overstreet, and Santos (2016)
Better Todays. Better Tomorrows.	Better Todays. Better Tomorrows. for Children's Mental Health is an innovative adult education program focusing on the mental health of children and youth ages 10–24 at the Idaho State University Institute of Rural Health (ISU-IRH). The project has offered training to 10,000 people since its inception in 2000, with participants representing three-quarters of Idaho's school districts and virtually all counties. Since 2006, Better Todays has partnered with the Idaho Awareness to Action Youth Suicide Project funded by the Substance Abuse and Mental Health Services Administration (SAMHSA). Previous funders have included the Idaho Office of the Governor and the Idaho Department of Health and Welfare. The National Institute on Mental Health Outreach Partners Program provides guidance on current science through ISU-IRH. **Goals:** The goals are to train adult gatekeepers on the signs and symptoms of mental illness in children and youth, suicide risk assessment and intervention, the latest scientific information on childhood mental disorders, and the impacts of trauma on mental health. Reducing stigma about mental health issues and encouraging early intervention and treatment-seeking also are key goals. Better Todays offers trainings in and outside Idaho. A train the trainer program also can be scheduled out of state to allow your organization to offer Better Todays trainings in your area.	Jaycox, Morse, and Tanielian (2006)

TIPs: Best-Practice Resource Inventory		
Resource	**Description** *Note:* Some of the descriptions in this column are quoted directly from the listed resources.	**References**
Southwest Michigan Children's Trauma Assessment Center's School Intervention Project: Classroom Tools/Curriculum	This resource includes background information on trauma and trauma-informed principles and provides several trauma-informed lesson plans that can be adapted for use with different age groups.	Jaycox, Morse, and Tanielian (2006)
National Child Traumatic Stress Network's Empirically Supported Treatments and Promising Practices	An online resource bank of research-based articles around trauma in schools along with promising practices for trauma intervention that can be adapted and used by schools utilized by the National Child Traumatic Stress Network centers.	https://www.nctsn.org/ trauma-informed-care/ trauma-informed -systems/schools/nctsn -resources
How Schools Can Help Students Recover from Traumatic Experiences	This toolkit provides a menu of programs that schools can implement to help children recover from trauma, categorized by type of trauma.	http://www.rand.org/ content/dam/rand/pubs/ technical_reports/2006/ RAND_TR413.pdf
The Flexible Framework: Six Elements of School Operations Involved in Creating a Trauma-Sensitive School	The Flexible Framework is an organizational tool that enables schools and districts—in collaboration with families, local community organizations, and outside providers—to maintain a whole school focus as they create trauma sensitive schools. The Framework is organized according to six core operational functions of schools, each of which is critical to any effort that seeks to make school-wide changes. The Framework is also a tool for policymakers to use as they design laws and policies that affect schools. In Massachusetts, TLPI advocates to ensure that statewide education laws and policies are organized according to the Framework. Organizing school climate and student support initiatives by these six core operational functions allows educators to align new initiatives, find efficiencies, and ensure all efforts in the school reinforce each other.	https://trauma sensitiveschools.org/ trauma-and-learning/the -flexible-framework/
Building Resilience in Students Impacted by Adverse Childhood Experiences: A Whole-Staff Approach	This workbook-style resource shows K–12 educators how to make a whole-school change, where strategies are integrated from curb to classroom. Readers will learn how to integrate trauma-informed strategies into daily instructional practice through expanded focus on: • The different experiences and unique challenges of students impacted by ACEs in urban, suburban, and rural schools, including suicidal tendencies, cyberbullying, and drugs • Behavior as a form of communication and how to explicitly teach new behaviors • How to mitigate trauma and build innate resiliency through a read, reflect, and respond model	Romero and Robertson (2018)
Threat Assessment	Threat assessment is a set of strategies and procedures to help identify potential threats and the likelihood that they will occur. It is a key component of a trauma-informed school because it helps a community to recognize and respond to threats to prevent traumatic events from occurring.	http://trauma awareschools.org/ threatAssessment

Trauma-Informed Practices

(Continued)

TIPs: Best-Practice Resource Inventory (Continued)		
Resource	**Description** *Note:* Some of the descriptions in this column are quoted directly from the listed resources.	**References**
Helping Traumatized Children Learn (HTCL) Version 2	*Helping Traumatized Children Learn* (HTCL) Version 2 describes a process that any school can use to become trauma sensitive. It is organized around four essential questions. The process is designed to guide schools through a process of transforming their culture.	https://trauma sensitiveschools.org/ tlpi-publications/
The ChildTrauma Academy (Dr. Bruce Perry)	The mission of the ChildTrauma Academy is to help improve the lives of traumatized and maltreated children—by improving the systems that educate, nurture, protect and enrich these children.	Childtrauma.org
Trauma-Sensitive Schools	Integrating research on children's neurodevelopment and educational best practices, this important book will build the capacity of teachers and school administrators to successfully manage the behavior of children with symptoms of complex developmental trauma.	Craig (2015)
Fostering Resilient Learners: Strategies for Creating a Trauma-Sensitive Classroom	Grounded in research and the authors' experience working with trauma-affected students and their teachers, *Fostering Resilient Learners* will help you cultivate a trauma-sensitive learning environment for students across all content areas, grade levels, and educational settings.	Souers and Hall (2016)
Help for Billy: A Beyond Consequences Approach to Helping Challenging Children in the Classroom, by Heather Forbes	The Beyond Consequences Institute is absolutely committed to helping schools become trauma-informed to help the "Billys" of the classroom. Who are the Billys of the classroom? You know who Billy is . . . Billy is the student who does not "fit" into the standard academic mold. Billy can be of any gender, race, or from any background. Billy has traditionally been perceived as being a trouble maker, lazy, disrespectful, agitated, disobedient, or even aggressive or violent. Billy stays in a constant cycle of negativity and interventions seem to only marginally, at best, maintain his behavior instead of helping him thrive in the classroom. With the trauma-informed resources we offer, you'll find out how to change all of this for Billy and put an end to the negative cycle. It's just a matter of providing the right support, environment, and relationships. Become a trauma-informed school and see magic happen!	http://www.beyond consequences.com/ schools
PACE Model	The PACE Model is composed of Playfulness, Acceptance, Curiosity, and Empathy. PACE is a way of thinking, feeling, communicating, and behaving that aims to make a child feel safe.	https://ddpnetwork.org/ about-ddp/meant-pace/
Lost at School: Why Our Kids With Behavioral Challenges Are Falling Through the Cracks and How We Can Help Them	This book offers new strategies for working with behaviorally challenging students.	Greene (2009)

Section 4: Questions to Consider

What resources do you think would help with your implementation of this behavior initiative?

_____

_____

_____

_____

_____

_____

_____

Name one resource listed that you will investigate further and why.

_____

_____

_____

_____

_____

_____

_____

_____

_____

Trauma-Informed Practices

SOCIAL AND EMOTIONAL LEARNING

SECTION 1: THE *WHAT*—SOCIAL AND EMOTIONAL LEARNING (SEL)

We know from research that providing high-quality, evidence-based social and emotional learning in schools has resulted in improvements in academics, behavior, and attitudes towards self, others, and school. And we know from experience that when we truly understand ourselves and each other better, and have opportunities to interact positively and productively with others, we're more engaged and invested in our learning and our community. Social and emotional learning is critical to enabling all students to achieve their fullest potential in school and in life.

—Melissa Schlinger
Vice President of Programs and Practice, CASEL:
Collaborative for Academic, Social, and Emotional Learning

Simply put, social and emotional learning (SEL) is a structure designed to help students understand the relationship between emotions and behaviors in relation to their own self-worth, academic achievement, well-being, and ability to learn how to self-regulate and connect with others. However, there are some noteworthy variations in common SEL definitions and styles of implementation. Even given the variations, the intended outcomes for SEL implementation are similar.

Each chapter in Part II is divided into four sections that end with questions to help guide discussions with your teacher or leadership teams around each behavior initiative. As you navigate through this chapter, remember to use the Behavior Initiatives K-W-L strategy to help organize your learnings around SEL implementation, beginning with the purpose for implementing SEL and common definitions (i.e., the *what*).

Purpose for SEL

- Create a climate and culture conducive to learning
- Integrate social and emotional learning into teaching practices such as cooperative learning and project-based learning
- Integrate social and emotional learning across academic curricula
- Improve achievement
- Improve resiliency skills
- Develop students' self-awareness and self-management skills that are essential in school and life

- Demonstrate ethical decision-making skills in personal, school, and community contexts
- Improve student connectedness
- Improve student learning
- Increase prosocial behaviors
- Improve students' attitudes toward school
- Reduce depression and stress among students
- Improve mental health
- Improve social skills

Variations of SEL

Based on our experiences helping schools implement behavior initiatives and through our research findings, we have noticed that there are multiple definitions or variations of the six behavior initiatives outlined in this book. That can be overwhelming while you are trying to decide which behavior initiative is best for your school or district, so we outline three common definitions for each of the six behavior initiatives identified in this book, based on repeated mentions of them through the research and in the field. *Note:* If a definition you prefer is not cited in this section, it does not mean it is not a worthy definition to use. We just want to provide a few examples of common definitions to help educators better understand each behavior initiative. We strongly believe that school or district staff need to understand the *what* definition and the rest of the information in each of these chapters in order to make informed decisions about implementation.

THREE COMMON SEL DEFINITIONS

Common Definition 1: "Social and emotional learning enhances students' capacity to integrate skills, attitudes, and behaviors to deal effectively and ethically with daily tasks and challenges. CASEL's integrated framework promotes intrapersonal, interpersonal, and cognitive competence. There are five core competencies that can be taught in many ways across many settings."

Self-Awareness

- Identifying emotions
- Accurate self-perception
- Recognizing strengths
- Self-confidence
- Self-efficacy

Self-Management

- Impulse control
- Stress management
- Self-discipline
- Self-motivation
- Goal-setting
- Organizational skills

Social Awareness

- Perspective-taking
- Empathy
- Appreciating diversity
- Respect for others

Relationship Skills

- Communication
- Social engagement
- Relationship-building
- Teamwork

Responsible Decision-Making

- Identifying problems
- Analyzing situations
- Solving problems
- Evaluating
- Reflecting
- Ethical responsibility (https://casel.org/core-competencies/)

Sources: CASEL, https://casel.org/corecompetencies/ and Zins, Weissberg, et al., (2004).

(Continued)

SEL

(Continued)

Common Definition 2: "SEL involves fostering social and emotional competencies through explicit instruction and through student-centered learning approaches that help students engage in the learning process and develop analytical, communication, and collaborative skills (Friedlaender et al., 2014).

Common Definition 3: Social and emotional learning is an organizing framework that "emphasizes four areas: skills, context, development, and outcomes. . . . [T]the framework divides core SEL skills into three domains: cognitive regulation (including attention control, inhibitory control, working memory/planning, cognitive flexibility), emotional processes (including emotion knowledge/expression, emotion/behavior regulation, empathy/perspective-taking), and social/interpersonal skills (including understanding social cues, conflict resolution, prosocial behavior). These three domains and their associated skills are related to both short- and long-term outcomes related to academic achievement (e.g., grades, standardized tests), behavioral adjustment (e.g., getting along with others, solving conflicts, and exhibiting less aggression/fewer conduct problems), and emotional health and wellbeing (e.g., lower levels of depression and social isolation)" (Jones & Bouffard, 2012, cited in Jones et al., 2017, pp. 12–13).

In Chapter 1 of this book, we shared a snapshot of a SEL school as a reference. We also want to provide a before-and-after story to help reinforce the beliefs and behaviors necessary for implementing SEL in your school or district.

A BEFORE-AND-AFTER SEL STORY

Before SEL . . . teachers were adamant about not teaching social and emotional learning skills in their classrooms. They complained that they already had enough to do and this is just one more thing. The majority of the teachers were convinced that parents should be teaching these skills and it was not their job. So as a result, if students did not get along or have a disagreement in their classrooms, exclusionary methods were utilized to address the problem instead of teaching students how to have empathy and compassion for other points of view and work together. Teachers voiced their fears in responding to social and emotional learning topics in their classrooms and especially voiced the fact that they were not comfortable with discussing such matters or addressing such conflicts in their classrooms in this manner.

After SEL . . . there was an intentional focus on teaching teachers how to embed social and emotional learning skills into what they were already doing in their classroom to take away the fear and frustration in implementation. They were provided with adequate training and ongoing supports to work with students on self-regulation, self-management, and relationship skills in every classroom and throughout the school. As a result, students began to understand that the culture of the school and classroom was around being inclusive and working together rather than being exclusive and punitive in nature. For example, teachers began to help students develop and follow classroom and group-based project norms in every classroom. Specifically, the focus of the norms was on how to work with diverse points of views/perspectives, diverse behaviors, and learn ways to problem solve, work together, and make responsible decisions when conflict or disagreements arose. In this norm system, there was also an opportunity for students to ask for additional teacher support when they felt as if they needed assistance in problem solving the issue.

Section 1: Questions to Consider

What are the intended outcomes of your school's or district's SEL initiative?

_____

_____

_____

_____

_____

_____

_____

_____

_____

How does your school or district define SEL?

_____

_____

_____

_____

_____

_____

_____

_____

_____

_____

(Continued)

(Continued)

What is currently in place at your school or district?

_____

_____

_____

_____

_____

_____

_____

_____

_____

_____

_____

_____

_____

_____

What would your next steps be, given what you have read so far?

_____

_____

_____

_____

_____

_____

_____

_____

_____

_____

_____

_____

_____

SECTION 2: CONNECTION TO HATTIE'S EFFECT SIZES IN RELATION TO THE CORE COMPONENTS OF SEL

Why Hattie's Effect Sizes?

In looking at what information about SEL would be helpful for educators, we went back to the question of what works best in education. That question also drove Hattie's comprehensive meta-analysis of areas that contribute to learning: the student, the home, the school, the classroom, the curricula, the teacher, and teaching and learning approaches (Hattie, 2018). Along with providing information on the relative effects of these influences on student achievement, Hattie also emphasized the importance of understanding and making visible the story of the underlying data. One of his most critical findings was how important it is to make teaching and learning visible. We agree and feel the same about making the teaching and learning of *behavior* visible. We've compared key components of SEL to influences Hattie identifies that impact student achievement. We feel these components are intrinsically linked to supporting a student's social emotional needs, and provide further evidence of the *why*; that is, implementation of these behavior initiatives is also critical to supporting a student's academic achievement. The following definition of key terms and description of how to interpret effect sizes will be a useful reference as you review the SEL table in this section.

HOW TO INTERPRET EFFECT SIZES

Hattie's work is based on achievement outcomes, while this book focuses on behaviors. We know that misbehavior can take away from students' achievement outcomes. A 1.0 standard deviation is typically associated with an increase in student achievement by two to three years. An effect size of 1.0 would mean that, on average, students receiving that treatment would exceed 84 percent of students not receiving the treatment. Hattie (2009) sets the benchmark of an effect size of $d = 0.4$ as the "hinge-point" where anything above it is labeled in the "zone of desired effects" as influences with the greatest impact on student learning. That doesn't mean that anything below 0.4 shouldn't be explored in greater detail. It just means that the influences aren't as great. Effects between $d = 0.15$ and $d = 0.40$ are typically what teachers could accomplish across an ordinary year of teaching. Ninety-five percent of everything we do has a positive influence on achievement, so setting the benchmark at anything above zero would be pointless. Furthermore, the zone between $d = 0.0$ and $d = 0.15$ is what students could achieve without schooling or by the simple process of maturation alone. Therefore, any effects below $d = 0.15$ are potentially harmful and should not be implemented. The remaining 5 percent of the factors have reverse effects, or decrease achievement. To put it simply, Hattie (2009) says that "students who do not achieve at least 0.40 improvement in a year are going backwards" (p. 250). Additionally, "It is a teacher who does not achieve an average of $d > 0.40$ per year that I do not want my children to experience" (p. 126).

Hattie presents his research through seven main contributors to learning (referred to as sources of influence): *the student, curricula, home, school, classroom, teacher, and teaching and learning approaches.* Hattie works through each of these sources of influence to evaluate which specific innovations and influences (factors) have the greatest impact on achievement. The factors are grouped by more specific "aspects" of each source of influence.

Visualize it like this:

1. **Student (*source of influence*)**
   a. Motivation & mental state (*aspect*)
      i. Depression (*factor*) (effect size [*d*] = –0.36)

2. **School (*source of influence*)**
   a. Leadership (*aspect*)
      i. School climate (*factor*) (*d* = 0.32)

The data in the table are listed from lowest effect size to highest. Remember, each source of influence is the broader category, and the subsets of each source are the aspects, which then group the various factors for each subset.

SEL: Connection to Hattie's Effect Sizes in Relation to the Core Components of This Behavior Initiative			
Source of Influence	Aspect	Factor	Effect Size
Student	Motivation & mental state	Depression	−0.36
School	Other school effects	Suspending or expelling students	−0.2
Student	Motivation & mental state	Lack of stress	0.17
Student	Beliefs, attitudes, dispositions	Mindfulness	0.29
School	Leadership	School climate	0.32
Curricula	Other curricula programs	Motivation/character programs	0.34
Classroom	Classroom influences	Decreasing disruptive behavior	0.34
Curricula	Play programs	Social skills program	0.4
Student	Motivation & mental state	Reducing anxiety	0.42
Teacher	Teacher-student interactions	Teacher-student relationships	0.52
Teaching: student learning strategies	Meta-cognition/self regulated learning	Self-regulation strategies	0.52

Source: Hattie, J. (2018, October). *Visible Learning^plus 250+ influences on student achievement.* Retrieved from https://us.corwin.com/sites/default/files/250_influences_10.1.2018.pdf. Retrieved February 4, 2019.

Educators tend to focus on the influences that have the most positive effects on student learning (those at the bottom of the preceding list), using that information to decide what to do more of. They don't generally look at the top of the list to identify what to do less of. Understanding this list from a strength and deficit lens allows educators to become more cognizant of the factors they influence directly, allowing them to target the effects these influences have on learning (e.g., by continuing, decreasing, or ending altogether certain practices) in order to create environments that reverse negative effects and increase positive effects on student success.

For example, depression has a −0.36 effect size on student achievement, which equates to a negative (or reverse) effect on learning. Knowing the negative effect that suffering from a mental state of depression has on student achievement, administrators can create a strong social emotional learning environment for students to improve student connectedness and increase prosocial behaviors.

We encourage you to use this information to help guide implementation of behavior initiatives.

Section 2: Questions to Consider

What connections can you make between the effect sizes of the common components of implementation of SEL and academic achievement?

_____

_____

_____

_____

_____

How will you use effect sizes to ask questions that will allow you to dig deeper to improve practice?

How will you use this information with your colleagues to achieve the desired outcomes for students?

SECTION 3: SYNTHESIZED INDICATORS OF SEL IMPLEMENTATION SUCCESS AND CHALLENGES

To develop this synthesized list of indicators of SEL implementation success and challenges, we relied on our research and experiences as practitioners. Specifically, we used a combination of peer-reviewed research findings, practical application and experiences from the field, and expert testimonials as our reference to identify common implementation success trends and challenge trends. We wanted to provide this information as you consider implementation of this behavior initiative.

SEL: Synthesized Indicators of Implementation Success and Challenges	
Implementation Success Trends	**Implementation Challenge Trends**
Adult beliefs and behaviors	Negative adult beliefs and behaviors
Clear and consistent messaging of SEL implementation and expectations	Policies not aligned with implementation
High expectations for students	Lack of clear understanding of the *why* around SEL
Encouraging student goal setting	Insufficient amount of time allotted for SEL
Policies aligned with SEL implementation	Teachers feeling overwhelmed
Whole-school approach	Lack of training
All-staff trainings (ongoing and relevant)	No system in place for progress monitoring implementation
Provide supports for SEL needs of staff and students	Lack of community and family partnerships
Encourage student voice and self-concept	Lack of consistency
Focus on developing key social and emotional skills across all grade levels and developmental needs	Lack of communication
	Lack of collaborative approach
Safe and welcoming environment	School structures and set up do not support SEL implementation
Established short- and long-term goals for implementation	Messaging that SEL is just a set of lessons
Build community and family partnerships	

Section 3: Question to Consider

To what extent will you use the synthesized indicators of implementation success and challenges to prevent obstacles during implementation?

_____

_____

_____

_____

_____

_____

_____

SECTION 4: SEL BEST-PRACTICE RESOURCE INVENTORY

To develop this best-practice resource inventory for SEL implementation, we again used as our reference points a combination of research and best practices in the field based on our experiences. For example, we included effective resources based on (1) peer-reviewed research findings and (2) data from schools and districts implementing SEL with effective outcomes for students. This information could be used as a starting point for looking into best-practice resources to assist with your implementation of SEL. *Note:* We understand that other resources are available. What is provided here is what we found based on the aforementioned criteria for this best-practice resource inventory.

SEL: Best-Practice Resource Inventory		
Resource	**Description** *Note:* Some of the descriptions in this column are quoted directly from the listed resources.	**References**
CASEL District-Level SEL	District-level SEL implementation guidelines and resource webinar.	https://casel.org/in-the-district/
The PATHS Program	The PATHS program is grounded in social and emotional learning (SEL). SEL helps children: • resolve conflicts peacefully • handle emotions positively • empathize • make responsible decisions.	https://www.channing-bete.com/prevention-programs/paths/paths.html
Second Step	Second Step is a program rooted in social-emotional learning (SEL) that helps transform schools into supportive, successful learning environments uniquely equipped to help children thrive. Second Step Social-Emotional Learning (SEL) gives students the tools to excel in and out of the classroom. Our easy-to-teach program garners outstanding reviews from educators who've noticed schoolwide improvement and see even the most challenging students make progress in emotion management, situational awareness, and academic achievement.	http://www.secondstep.org/
First Step to Success	First Step to Success is an early intervention program designed to help children who are at risk for developing aggressive or antisocial behavioral patterns. The program uses a trained behavior coach who works with each student and his or her class peers, teacher, and parents for approximately 50 to 60 hours over a three-month period. First Step to Success includes three interconnected modules: screening, classroom intervention, and parent training. The screening module is used to identify candidates who meet eligibility criteria for program participation. Classroom intervention and parent training comprise the program intervention component of First Step to Success.	http://firststeptosuccess.org/

SEL

(Continued)

SEL: Best-Practice Resource Inventory (Continued)		
Resource	Description *Note:* Some of the descriptions in this column are quoted directly from the listed resources.	References
Conscious Discipline	Conscious Discipline is a comprehensive emotional intelligence and classroom management system that integrates all domains of learning (social, emotional, physical, cultural and cognitive) into one seamless curriculum. It evolves from constantly asking, "Is there a better way," and seeking the most current information provided by varied disciplines from neuroscience to mindfulness research to developmental psychology and beyond.	https://consciousdiscipline.com/
RULER Approach	The RULER Approach to Social and Emotional Learning is a school-wide approach designed for use in kindergarten through eighth grade to promote emotional literacy, which includes Recognizing, Understanding, Labeling, Expressing, and Regulating emotions (the "RULER" skills). RULER implementation involves systematic professional development for the adults involved in the education of children (school leaders, teachers, support staff, and families) so that emotions become central to learning, teaching, and parenting. In the first year, teachers learn and then teach the "anchors" of emotional literacy: four tools that were designed to help both adults and students to develop their RULER skills, self- and social awareness, empathy, and perspective-taking ability, as well as to foster a healthy emotional climate. Subsequently teachers learn how to integrate the approach into their standard curriculum and experience The Feeling Words Curriculum, a language-based emotional literacy program for students. In addition, RULER has an interactive training program designed to provide adult family members with strategies for extending and promoting social and emotional development at home. Initial training for RULER typically lasts at least two days and is required. RULER offers a train-the-trainer system to support sustainability.	http://ei.yale.edu/ruler/ruler-overview/
Navigating SEL from Inside and Out	This report is the product of a detailed content analysis of 25 leading SEL and character education programs commissioned by the Wallace Foundation and conducted by a research team at the Harvard Graduate School Education led by Dr. Stephanie Jones.	Jones et al. (2017)
The 4Rs Program	The 4Rs program (Reading, Writing, Respect, and Resolution) provides read-alouds, book talks, and sequential, interactive skills lessons to develop social and emotional skills related to understanding and managing feelings, listening and developing empathy, being assertive, solving conflict creatively and nonviolently, honoring diversity, and standing up to teasing and bullying. 4Rs is a grade-specific program available for students in prekindergarten through eighth grade. Divided into seven units, each grade has approximately 35 lessons—one a week throughout the year. Units also include extension activities, infusion ideas, recommendations of other books, and 4Rs Activity Sheets to reinforce students' understanding. The 4Rs program reinforces skills and concepts covered in each unit with a Family Connection activity that students take home to complete with their caregivers and 4Rs "Family Connections" parent workshops. Peer Mediation and Peace Helper programs are also available to support classroom- and school-wide programming. All 4Rs stories incorporate a variety of cultures, ethnicities, and backgrounds. Initial training for the 4Rs program typically lasts 25–30 hours and is required. 4Rs offers a train-the-trainer system to support sustainability.	https://www.morningsidecenter.org/4rs-program

SEL: Best-Practice Resource Inventory		
Resource	**Description** *Note:* Some of the descriptions in this column are quoted directly from the listed resources.	**References**
MindUP	The MindUP program provides separate sets of lessons for three levels: prekindergarten through second grade; third through fifth grade; and sixth through eighth grade. Beginning after the third lesson, MindUP establishes core practices of deep breathing and attentive listening, which are then practiced several times a day throughout the school year. These practices are designed to enhance students' self awareness, focus attention, promote self-regulation, and reduce stress. In addition there are 15 structured lessons at each level that span four units. Each lesson provides an explanation of how the content and objective of the lesson is supported by brain research. The lessons also include a "getting ready" activity, a MindUP warm-up, and detailed instructions to the teacher on how to engage students and support their exploration and reflection on the topic. In addition, there are suggestions for creating an "optimistic classroom." Throughout, the program works to promote generalization and support connections to academic instruction, and there are suggested lesson extensions to support social and emotional development, mathematics, physical education, health, science, literature, and journal writing. MindUP offers suggestions to support English Language Learners. Initial training for the MindUP program typically lasts one full day (seven hours), and regional and collaborative workshops last two to two and one-half days. Training is not required, and MindUP offers a train-the-trainer system to support sustainability.	https://mindup.org/
SECURe	SECURe: Social, Emotional, and Cognitive Understanding and Regulation in Education resources	https://easel.gse.harvard.edu/secure
Responsive Classroom	Responsive Classroom is an approach to teaching based on the belief that integrating academic and social-emotional skills creates an environment where students can do their best learning. The Responsive Classroom approach consists of a set of practices and strategies that build academic and social-emotional competencies. This approach works well with many other programs and can be introduced gradually into a teacher's practice. The Responsive Classroom approach is informed by the work of educational theorists and the experiences of exemplary classroom teachers. Six principles guide this approach: 1. Teaching social and emotional skills is as important as teaching academic content. 2. How we teach is as important as what we teach. 3. Great cognitive growth occurs through social interaction. 4. How we work together as adults to create a safe, joyful, and inclusive school environment is as important as our individual contribution or competence. 5. What we know and believe about our students—individually, culturally, developmentally—informs our expectations, reactions, and attitudes about those students. 6. Partnering with families—knowing them and valuing their contributions—is as important as knowing the children we teach.	https://www.responsiveclassroom.org/

(Continued)

SEL

SEL: Best-Practice Resource Inventory (Continued)		
Resource	Description *Note:* Some of the descriptions in this column are quoted directly from the listed resources.	References
I Can Problem Solve	Formally called Interpersonal Cognitive Problem Solving (also ICPS) . . . an evidence-based, universal primary prevention program that helps children, as early as age four, learn: • **Perspective-taking**—awareness and sensitivity to people's feelings • **Alternative solution thinking**—ability to generate a variety of solutions to interpersonal problems • **Consequential thinking**—ability to recognize the impact of one's behavior upon others, in light of what might happen next In addition, beginning at age eight, ICPS helps children learn more sophisticated thinking skills such as: • **Recognizing mixed emotions**—ability to feel opposite ways about the same thing • **Understanding motives**—recognition of various possible reasons people act the way they do • **Means-end thinking**—ability to plan sequenced steps toward a goal, recognizing obstacles that might interfere with reaching that goal and that it takes time to reach a goal By teaching children how to think, not what to think, the program changes thinking styles and, as a result, enhances children's social adjustment, promotes pro-social behaviors and prevents negative, impulsive and withdrawn behaviors.	http://www.ican problemsolve.info/
Lions Quest	Lions Quest PreK–12 programs use a social and emotional learning (SEL) curriculum to teach character education, drug and bullying prevention, and service-learning through comprehensive lesson plans that educators use in the classroom. Our programs work. They help young people become better students, better decision makers, and better citizens.	https://www.lions-quest.org/
Open Circle	Classroom teachers implement the grade-differentiated Open Circle Curriculum during twice-weekly, 15-minute Open Circle Meetings. Students form a circle of chairs, including an empty seat to symbolize that there is always room for another person, voice or opinion. Open Circle Meetings are also a familiar and safe setting for children to discuss important issues in their classroom, school, local community or the broader world. Open Circle lessons are highly interactive, incorporating large and small group discussions, role playing, community-building and mindfulness activities and practices, and high quality children's literature. Teachers and counselors also use the Open Circle Curriculum in their work with students who require additional, targeted instruction. The Open Circle Curriculum is designed for implementation by current and past participants in Open Circle's Classroom Teacher Program.	https://www.open-circle.org/

SEL: Best-Practice Resource Inventory		
Resource	**Description** *Note:* Some of the descriptions in this column are quoted directly from the listed resources.	**References**
The Whole School, Whole Community, Whole Child (WSCC)	The Whole School, Whole Community, Whole Child (WSCC) model is the next evolution of the traditional coordinated school health approach. Developed by ASCD and the U.S. Centers for Disease Control and Prevention (CDC) and launched in spring 2014, the model aims to better align the policies, processes, and practices of education, public health, and school health, and in doing so, improve learning and health.	http://www.wholechild education.org/
"The Practice Base for How We Learn: Supporting Students' Social, Emotional, and Academic Development"	The Council of Distinguished Educators of the National Commission on Social, Emotional, and Academic Development has released a new consensus statement. "The Practice Base for How We Learn: Supporting Students' Social, Emotional, and Academic Development" outlines promising practices that show how students, teachers, parents, and administrators can integrate social, emotional, and academic learning in PreK–12 education. The report examines how both the teacher and the school environment need to support the social, emotional, and academic dimensions of learning to maximize the outcomes for all students.	https://assets.aspen institute.org/content/ uploads/2018/03/CDE -Practice-Base_FINAL.pdf
All Learning Is Social and Emotional: Helping Students Develop Essential Skills for the Classroom and Beyond	This book is a comprehensive, five-part model of SEL that's easy to integrate into everyday content instruction, no matter what subject or grade level you teach. You'll learn the *hows* and *whys* of 1. Building students' sense of identity and confidence in their ability to learn, overcome challenge, and influence the world around them. 2. Helping students identify, describe, and regulate their emotional responses. 3. Promoting the cognitive regulation skills critical to decision making and problem solving. 4. Fostering students' social skills, including teamwork and sharing, and their ability to establish and repair relationships. 5. Equipping students to becoming informed and involved citizens.	Frey, Fisher, and Smith (2019)
Handbook of Social and Emotional Learning: Research and Practice	This handbook offers a comprehensive overview of the current research, practice, and policy in the SEL field.	Durlak, Domitrovich, Weissberg, and Gullotta (2015)
From a Nation at Risk to a Nation at Hope: Recommendations from the National Commission on Social, Emotional, & Academic Development	This website, designed to help a growing movement dedicated to the social, emotional, and academic well-being of children, is reshaping learning and changing lives across America. Includes resources, videos, reports, and best practices to guide implementation of SEL in schools.	http://nationathope.org/ report-from-the-nation/

SEL

Section 4: Questions to Consider

What resources do you think would help with your implementation of this behavior initiative?

_____

_____

_____

_____

_____

_____

_____

_____

Name one resource listed that you will investigate further and why.

_____

_____

_____

_____

_____

_____

_____

_____

_____

Chapter 8 is designed to help you decide which behavior initiatives fit your district's or school's needs and your action plan implementation.

BUILDING BEHAVIOR
(The *How*)

PART THREE

BRINGING IT ALL TOGETHER

Building Behavior Initiatives

IN THIS CHAPTER you will find the processes and tools you will need to bring all the information in this book together and begin the difficult but meaningful work around building behavior initiatives at your school.

Section 1: Bringing It All Together: Synthesis of the Six Behavior Initiatives

Section 2: SchoolWide Behavior Initiatives Process (SW-BIP)

Section 3: Closing Thoughts: Tips and Suggestions From the Authors

SECTION 1: BRINGING IT ALL TOGETHER: SYNTHESIS OF THE SIX BEHAVIOR INITIATIVES

In our synthesis of the vast amount of information surrounding this topic, we found more commonalities than differences among the six behavior initiatives identified in this book. The number-one factor for success in effective implementation for *all* six of the behavior initiatives was related to the *belief in the adults implementing them* (understanding the *why* and the purpose) and the number-one reason for implementation challenges was *lack of fidelity in implementation* (no systemic audit of student needs and utilization based on best practices).

With that said, it is essential for schools and districts to understand the *why*, the *what*, and the *how* around the implementation of behavior initiatives at the districtwide or schoolwide level. In this chapter, you will find a graphic organizer that connects each of the six behavior initiatives highlighted in this book. The "Six Behavior Initiatives at a Glance" graphic (Figure 8.1) provides a snapshot of the commonalities (center of the graphic) along with some key focuses or components of each of the behavior initiatives. In other words, some critical distinctions (separate boxes for each initiative) will present certain areas of emphasis for you when considering which behavior initiatives will yield the best results for your school or district and/or act as your starting point. You will find that all six of the behavior initiatives are rooted in providing students equitable access to their education in a positive and inclusive culture/environment and in preparing students to be productive members of their community, society, and world.

Thoughts resonating with you so far:

_____

_____

_____

_____

_____

_____

_____

_____

_____

_____

_____

FIGURE 8.1 ■ Six Behavior Initiatives at a Glance

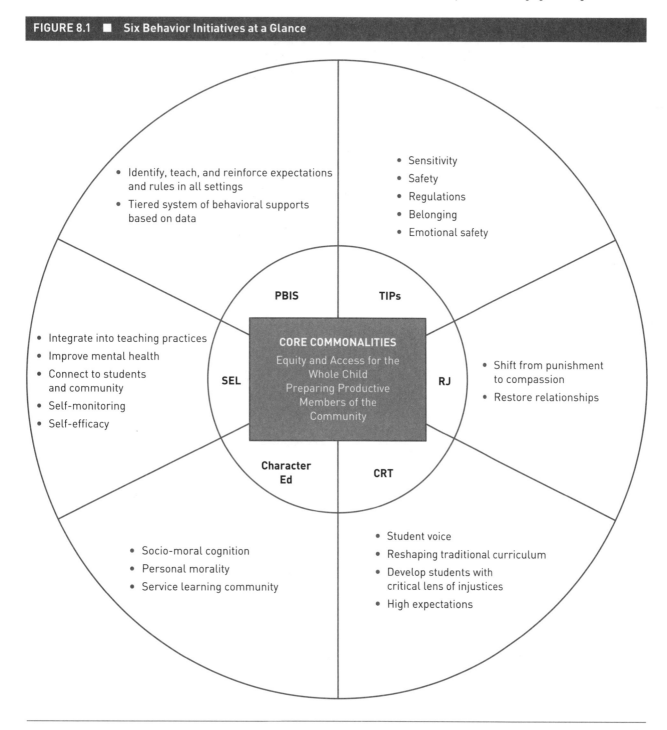

In Part I of this book, we asked you to use the Behavior Initiatives K-W-L (Know, Want to Know, Learned) strategy as you read about each behavior initiative (see Figure 1.3). The purpose of this strategy was to help you access prior or background knowledge of each behavior initiative, synthesize the information, compare and contrast commonalities and differences, but, most important, understand the purpose, definitions, impact, and best-practice resources for implementation of each behavior initiative to help make informed decisions about what your students need.

Now that you have learned about each of the six behavior initiatives in this book, you will go through a process for deciding which initiative or combination of initiatives is best for your school or district and why. Even if you have a behavior initiative in place that you feel is working for your school or district, continue this process to help build on it based on the best-practice information shared in this book. Before you do that, however, let's check for understanding of each behavior initiative by matching sample problem statements with the behavior initiatives that represent a possible good fit or match for addressing the problem.

Sample Problem Statement	Behavior Initiative Representing a Possible Good Fit or Match
A majority of the students have experienced trauma according to ACEs.	Trauma-informed practices (Chapter 6)
The school needs consistent rules, procedures, and expectations for all students and all classrooms.	Positive behavior interventions and supports (Chapter 2)
Students are struggling to understand or self-regulate their emotions or responding to others.	Social and emotional learning (Chapter 7)
A high number of repeat offenses take place with strictly punitive and exclusionary practices being used.	Restorative justice (Chapter 4)
Students are not making a connection between their behaviors and how those behaviors impact their future.	Character education (Chapter 3)
Students feel like they do not have a voice in their education. Teachers are not considering the students' culture in their teaching.	Culturally responsive teaching (Chapter 5)

These are just a handful of examples to help you. We encourage you to identify additional problem statements as you continue reading this part of the book.

Thoughts resonating with you so far:

_____

_____

_____

_____

_____

_____

_____

List some possible problem statements and a possible good fit or match based on your readings . . .	
Sample Problem Statement	Behavior Initiative Representing a Possible Good Fit or Match

Multiple Behavior Initiatives

As mentioned earlier, some schools and districts may decide to implement multiple behavior initiatives based on their students' needs. Based on our findings and practitioner lens, we do not see a problem with that as long as the initiatives are working hand in hand and around a common goal and are not competing initiatives. Allow yourself to find success with one first and then weave in another, rather than beginning with pieces of several initiatives. All of these behavior initiatives have a place in our schools as long as implementation decisions are made and supported based on students' needs. What helps us conceptualize implementation toward staff buy-in is comparing the behavioral initiatives to the academic initiatives in place at your school and district. For example, saying that only one behavior initiative will benefit our students would be like saying our students will respond to only one instructional strategy (e.g., project-based learning), rather than a combination of scaffolding *and* project-based learning. Why should it be any different for behavior initiatives? A combination of behavior initiatives will better support our students' social and emotional learning much in the same way a combination of instructional strategies would better support their academic learning. One note of caution, though: Implement one behavior initiative with full fidelity before you blend another initiative into your school or district, if possible.

See what we mean in the following brief sample scenarios of schools that had a strong foundation for multiple initiatives.

Critical note: *Behavior initiatives do not need to be in competition with each other; they can build on each other.*

Multiple Behavior Initiatives Scenario	Implementation Approach
Elementary School A was having difficulty blending character education and PBIS. They did not want to get rid of character education but wanted to embed the PBIS structure.	The leadership team decided to keep both initiatives and make it work with clear expectations. They called their SOAR PBIS expectations "Self-control, On task, Achievement, and Respect—SOAR with Character!" **Tier 1:** "SOAR with Character!" was highlighted every month with a character trait and a poster/writing prompt in all classrooms. **Tier 2:** Peer mediators trained to help students demonstrate SOAR. Peer mediators also taught lessons to all students on important peer mediation skills. **Tier 3:** Students who were having challenges were given the option to be a part of peer mediation to help them apply skills.
Middle School B had been implementing PBIS for several years but wanted to add restorative justice practices based on the needs of their students.	Instead of this becoming a competing initiative, they decided on what restorative justice looks like in each tier of PBIS implementation at their school site: **Tier 1:** All classrooms developed and posted a Respect Agreement. **Tier 2:** Teachers were trained on using restorative classroom contracts with students. **Tier 3:** Student court was used.
District C had begun the work of developing an SEL behavior initiative districtwide but realized they also wanted a structure for PBIS in place to help systematize the implementation in a tiered approach.	Instead of SEL being selected over PBIS, the district leadership team decided how they were going to prioritize and align both initiatives districtwide with clear expectations for rollout: **Tier 1:** SEL critical components taught in every classroom, with lessons prepared and training provided. **Tier 2:** Small group or individual teaching of the six critical components based on student need. **Tier 3:** One-to-one SEL support and plan for the student, including use of a mental health component to master critical components.

SECTION 2: SCHOOLWIDE BEHAVIOR INITIATIVES PROCESS (SW-BIP)

This section describes the SchoolWide Behavior Initiatives Process (SW-BIP). It is up to you to determine the lens you want to use as you go through this process. Similar to how individual students may need a behavior intervention plan based on the function(s) of their behavior and social and emotional needs, the same has to happen at the school or district level based on the needs of the students in the school or district. Consider the SW-BIP a schoolwide process that requires stakeholder input to develop, implement, and adjust as needed based on responses to the initiatives and as measured by goal attainment.

FIGURE 8.2 ■ Three Phases of the SW-BIP

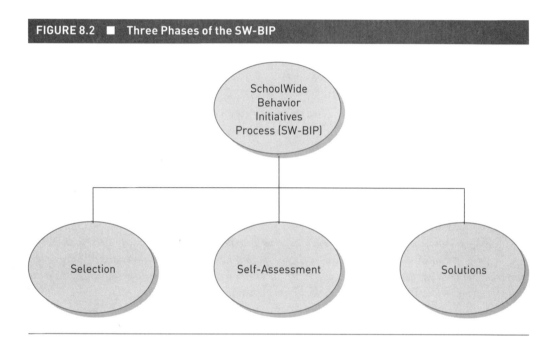

The SW-BIP is divided into three phases (see Figure 8.2) and designed to guide schools or districts through effective implementation of behavior initiatives:

Phase 1—Selection. Selecting behavior initiatives or re-evaluating existing behavior initiatives to implement based on data (see Figure 8.3)

Phase 2—Self-assessment. Completing a rating scale to guide a site or district-level leadership team to delve more deeply into components necessary for effective implementation (see Figure 8.4)

Phase 3—Solutions. Embedding the five whys and fishbone processes as the school or district identifies next step actions and timelines (see Figure 8.5)

SW-BIP PHASE 1: SELECTION

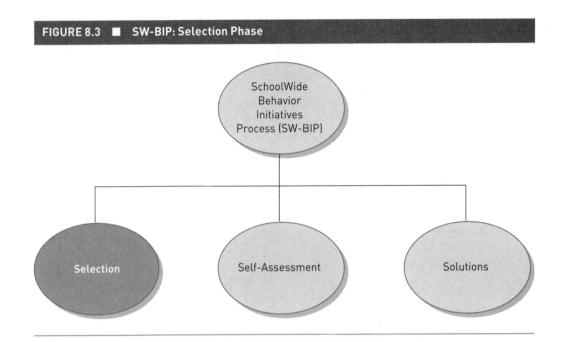

FIGURE 8.3   ■   SW-BIP: Selection Phase

What Happens in the Selection Phase? *The objective in this phase is to identify the behavior initiative that best fits your school, based on what you have learned about the initiatives in this book and what you know of your school's needs according to stakeholder input and student data. Select one behavior initiative to begin. You can repeat this process for other behavior initiatives. Answer the three questions in the Behavior Initiative Selection Guide based on stakeholder input and student data for the behavior initiative you selected. Continue the three-question process three times, considering multiple stakeholder feedback (i.e., teacher stakeholders, community stakeholders and student data). The intended outcome is to use your new learning in addition to stakeholder input and student data to make an informed decision and justify the* why *behind choosing the selected behavior initiative to implement at your school.*

Note: If you already have a behavior initiative in place at your school, use your existing behavior initiative through this process and make sure it matches the stakeholder needs and student data.

Data Finding Tip: If you are struggling identifying what type of data to use in this phase, use the following table as a guide:

Quantitative Data Examples	Qualitative Data Examples
Demographics, ethnicity, gender, school characteristics	Interviews, observations, climate surveys (open-ended)
Teacher and specialist qualifications	Classroom environment visits, visuals and celebrations
Student performance, promotion rates, grades, AP scores	MTSS descriptions (criteria for entrance and exit)
Drop-out rates	Stakeholder focus groups (students, staff, community)
Student engagement, attendance, school involvement	Discipline practice and process descriptions
Suspensions, detentions, expulsions	Intervention referral practice and process descriptions
Culture and climate survey (students, staff, community)	

Quantitative Data Examples	Qualitative Data Examples
Social and emotional interventions and programs offered	Evidence of universal design for learning
Number of students receiving special education services	Mission/Vision/Values/Beliefs
Number of students receiving 504 accommodations	Clear school SMART goals (academic and behavior)
Number of students on individualized behavior/SEL supports	School site plan
	Local control accountability plan

Behavior Initiative Selection Guide: Culturally Responsive Teaching Sample

Behavior Initiative 3 × 3 Selection Guide

Insert the schoolwide behavior initiative you would like to implement or improve implementation of based on your new learning: Culturally Responsive Teaching

Instructions: Answer the three questions considering multiple stakeholder input and student data for the behavior initiative you selected to put through this 3 × 3 selection process. Continue the three-question process for each stakeholder group. The intended outcome is to use your new learning and match it to stakeholder input and student data needs to make an informed decision and justify the why behind choosing this particular behavior initiative.

Name of Selected Behavior Initiative 3 × 3 process	1. Based on input data from each stakeholder group, why do you think this behavior initiative best fits your school?	2. What are some best-practice resources that can help you design implementation based on input data from each stakeholder group?	3. What are the intended outcomes for implementing this behavior initiative?
Initiative 1. Culturally responsive teaching	The school has diversified based on the new boundary changes. Stakeholder group: leadership team	Teaching Tolerance website	Educate staff on the *why* (meaning and strategies) connected to culturally responsive practices.
Initiative 2. Culturally responsive teaching	Key community stakeholders have reported in school surveys that they do not feel welcomed by the teachers. Stakeholder group: community members	*The Dreamkeepers: Successful Teachers of African-American students*, 2nd ed.	Educate and model for teachers how to establish a welcoming classroom and school environment.
Initiative 3. Culturally responsive teaching	Students are feeling like they do not have a say in their learning and that the teachers do not understand them based on student perception surveys. Stakeholder group: students	7 Principles for Culturally Responsive Teaching	Educate staff on best practices for establishing culturally responsive practices.

Additional Notes/Comments:

- Formal training is needed.

- We need to make sure we have aligned our funding for professional development opportunities around this selected initiative.

Behavior Initiative 3 × 3 Selection Guide

Insert the schoolwide behavior initiative you would like to implement or improve implementation of based on your new learning: _____

Instructions: Answer the three questions considering multiple stakeholder input and student data for the behavior initiative you selected to put through this 3 × 3 selection process. Continue the three-question process for each stakeholder group. The intended outcome is to use your new learning and match it to stakeholder input and student data needs to make an informed decision and justify the why behind choosing this particular behavior initiative.

Name of Selected Behavior Initiative 3 × 3 process	1. Based on input data from each stakeholder group, why do you think this behavior initiative best fits your school?	2. What are some best practices resources that can help you design implementation based on input data from each stakeholder group?	3. What are your intended outcomes for wanting to implement this behavior initiative?
Initiative 1.	Stakeholder group:		
Initiative 2.	Stakeholder group:		
Initiative 3.	Stakeholder group:		
Additional Notes/Comments:			

SW-BIP PHASE 2: SELF-ASSESSMENT

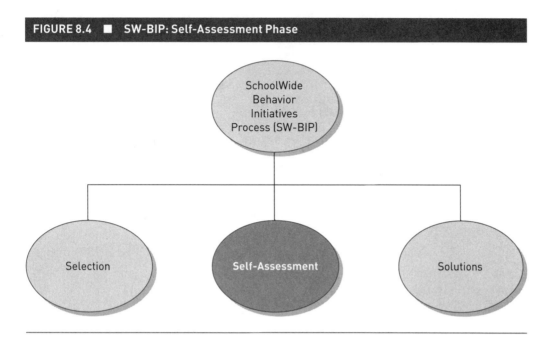

What Happens in the Self-Assessment Phase? *The objective in this phase is to assess the current state of your school's or district's implementation of the behavior initiative you selected in the selection phase. Complete either the schoolwide or districtwide version of the Behavior Initiative Self-Assessment with your leadership team. This team should have representation of key stakeholders.*

Note: This self-assessment is designed to assess implementation of one behavior initiative at a time. If you have multiple behavior initiatives, you will need to complete multiple behavior initiative self-assessments.

Note: We provide you with a district version of the assessment as well, in case you want to start there before assessing the school level, since they are so connected.

Thoughts resonating with you so far:

_____

_____

_____

_____

_____

_____

_____

Behavior Initiative Self-Assessment: Schoolwide Version

Instructions: Complete the self-assessment with key stakeholders. After each statement, circle the number that best indicates how you believe your school functions in its current state. 1 = strongly disagree, 2 = disagree, 3 = neither agree nor disagree, 4 = agree, 5 = strongly agree	If you scored 3 or lower on this item, identify how you will move your score to a 4 or a 5. What will be your evidence of proficiency?

Leadership (belief, competency, alignment, and supports)

1. There is a shared vision and mission around implementation of this schoolwide behavior initiative.

   1   2   3   4   5

2. There is alignment of the vision and mission with the school's top priority initiatives.

   1   2   3   4   5

3. A school team exists, comprised of administrators and specialized support services experts who meet at least monthly with the purpose of guiding and monitoring implementation of this behavior initiative through the use data and a problem-solving model.

   1   2   3   4   5

4. There is collective agreement around shared responsibility amongst the school-level team members coordinating this schoolwide behavior initiative.

   1   2   3   4   5

5. There is a clear understanding of the *why* for implementing the selected behavior initiative schoolwide.

   1   2   3   4   5

6. Implementing this behavior initiative schoolwide is one of the top priorities for the school and is understood by teachers and staff.

   1   2   3   4   5

Resources/Funding (resources/funding and alignment of goals and needs in all school settings)

7. Resources/funds are secured and allocated for implementation and training of this behavior initiative schoolwide.

   1   2   3   4   5

8. The school-level team has a general understanding of the current state of this behavior initiative implementation in all school settings.

   1   2   3   4   5

9. Adequate support services and/or special education human resource needs are met for successful implementation of the selected behavior initiative.

   1   2   3   4   5

10. Resources or additional supports for implementation are provided to teachers and staff in the school based on student needs.

   1   2   3   4   5

11. Additional funding and resources are allocated for ongoing training opportunities for new implementers.

   1   2   3   4   5

12. The school ensures funding is utilized equitably and accordingly.

   1   2   3   4   5

Professional Development (ongoing training and education opportunities)

13. There is a clear understanding of the best practices or critical components necessary for schoolwide implementation of the selected behavior initiative.

1	2	3	4	5

14. A plan exists to provide additional professional development and resources to teachers and staff having challenges with implementation of the selected behavior initiative.

1	2	3	4	5

15. A process exists to address misconceptions and challenges.

1	2	3	4	5

16. The school's parent clubs are educated on the reasons why and steps required for implementing behavior initiatives with fidelity.

1	2	3	4	5

17. School policies are aligned to the language supporting this behavior initiative implementation.

1	2	3	4	5

18. A schoolwide database allows for accurate progress monitoring of behavioral data from all settings.

1	2	3	4	5

Accountability (structure for progress monitoring, communication, and ongoing improvement)

19. Clear expectations are identified for this schoolwide behavior initiative implementation.

1	2	3	4	5

20. School-level SMART goals have been developed around implementation of the selected behavior initiative.

1	2	3	4	5

21. Short-term and long-term school-level SMART goals have been developed and are understood by district- and site-level implementers of this behavior initiative.

1	2	3	4	5

22. Progress monitoring procedures are in place to measure proficiency around schoolwide implementation of this behavior initiative with clear timelines and communication for improvement identified.

1	2	3	4	5

23. Multiple methods are in place for data collection and stakeholder feedback to assess the current behavioral needs of students schoolwide.

1	2	3	4	5

24. Evidence of implementation is gathered quarterly from teachers and staff in the school by the school leadership team.

1	2	3	4	5

Total

Add the circled numbers, and record the total: _____

Goal = 96–120 points (80% or higher)

Behavior Initiative Self-Assessment: Districtwide Version

Instructions: Complete the self-assessment with key stakeholders. After each statement, circle the number that best indicates how you believe your school district functions in its current state.

1 = strongly disagree, 2 = disagree, 3 = neither agree nor disagree, 4 = agree, 5 = strongly agree

If you scored 3 or lower on this item, identify how you will move your score to a 4 or a 5.

What will be your evidence of proficiency?

Leadership (belief, competency, alignment, and supports)

1. There is a shared vision and mission around implementation of this districtwide behavior initiative.

   1   2   3   4   5

2. There is alignment of the vision and mission with the district's top priority initiatives.

   1   2   3   4   5

3. A district team exists, comprised of administrators and specialized support services experts who meet at least monthly with the purpose of guiding and monitoring implementation of this behavior initiative through the use data and a problem-solving model.

   1   2   3   4   5

4. There is collective agreement around shared responsibility amongst the district-level team coordinating this districtwide behavior initiative.

   1   2   3   4   5

5. There is a clear understanding of the *why* for implementing the selected behavior initiative districtwide.

   1   2   3   4   5

6. Implementing this behavior initiative districtwide is one of the top priorities for the district and is understood at every school site.

   1   2   3   4   5

Resources/Funding (resources/funding and alignment of goals and needs of each school)

7. Resources/funds are secured and allocated for implementation and training of this behavior initiative districtwide.

   1   2   3   4   5

8. The district-level team has a general understanding of the current state of this behavior initiative implementation at each school site.

   1   2   3   4   5

9. Adequate support services and/or special education human resource needs are met for successful implementation of the selected behavior initiative.

   1   2   3   4   5

10. Resources or additional supports for implementation are provided to schools in the district based on student needs.

    1   2   3   4   5

11. Additional funding and resources are allocated for ongoing training opportunities for new implementers.

    1   2   3   4   5

12. The district ensures funding is utilized equitably and accordingly.

    1   2   3   4   5

Professional Development (ongoing training and education opportunities)

13. There is a clear understanding of the best practices or critical components necessary for districtwide implementation of the selected behavior initiative.

1	2	3	4	5

14. A plan exists to provide additional professional development and resources to schools having challenges with implementation of the selected behavior initiative.

1	2	3	4	5

15. A process exists to address misconceptions and challenges.

1	2	3	4	5

16. The school board is educated on the reasons why and steps required for implementing behavior initiatives with fidelity.

1	2	3	4	5

17. District policies are aligned to the language supporting this behavior initiative implementation.

1	2	3	4	5

18. A districtwide database allows for accurate progress monitoring of behavioral data from each school site.

1	2	3	4	5

Accountability (structure for progress monitoring, communication, and ongoing improvement)

19. Clear expectations are identified for this districtwide behavior initiative implementation.

1	2	3	4	5

20. District-level SMART goals have been developed around implementation of the selected behavior initiative.

1	2	3	4	5

21. Short-term and long-term district-level SMART goals have been developed and are understood by district- and site-level implementers of this behavior initiative.

1	2	3	4	5

22. Progress monitoring procedures are in place to measure proficiency around districtwide implementation of this behavior initiative with clear timelines and communication for improvement identified.

1	2	3	4	5

23. Multiple methods are in place for data collection and stakeholder feedback to assess the current behavioral needs of students districtwide.

1	2	3	4	5

24. Evidence of implementation is gathered quarterly from each school site in the district by the district leadership team.

1	2	3	4	5

Total

Add the circled numbers, and record the total: _____

Goal = 96–120 points (80% or higher)

SW-BIP PHASE 3: SOLUTIONS

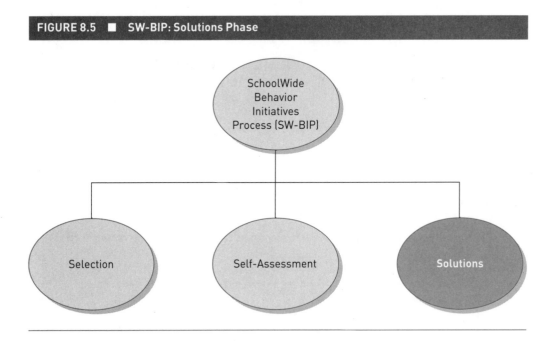

FIGURE 8.5   ■   SW-BIP: Solutions Phase

What Happens in the Solutions Phase? *The objective in this phase is to utilize the Behavior Initiative Self-Assessment results and other relevant information regarding implementation of the behavior initiative you selected and put the implementation through the following three-step solutions process:*

> ***Step 1.*** *Five whys analysis to get to the core of the problem and/or challenges around implementation*
>
> ***Step 2.*** *The fishbone process to identify the problem statement(s), possible root causes, and effects*
>
> ***Step 3.*** *Action plan based on Steps 1 and 2*

In simpler terms, the solutions phase is designed to prevent or address the common implementation chasm discussed in Part I of this book for the successful implementation of your chosen behavior initiative(s).

To demonstrate this phase of the SW-BIP process, we present a behavior initiative scenario to emphasize the common issues schools may face in implementing their selected behavior initiative and the factors that lead to the problems faced, preventing them from crossing the implementation chasm.

THE IMPLEMENTATION CHASM

Wilbur School recently went through a school boundary change. As a result, two new apartment complexes now feed into the school's traditionally high-income neighborhood. This new diversity has affected the culture of the school. According to the school's recent state assessment data, severe gaps exist between students of color and their white peers in terms of academic achievement and discipline. Staff claim the data are the result of the "new type of student" they have in their classrooms and blame the lack of proper instruction in the home or at the previous school, lack of parenting, and poor attendance for the significant spike in discipline and decline in achievement. Campus administrators are spreading the same sentiment, creating a disconnect between staff and the students and community. No effort is being made to invest in developing relationships with the students or community. Staff express that they are afraid to communicate with "these types of parents." To make matters worse, the majority of the staff regularly verbalize their discontent with the students.

Currently, teachers write referrals as the first step in their classroom discipline system without attempting other preventive or corrective interventions or responses. The school's discipline system overall appears to be failing. Teachers continue to give referrals with no follow up and at their own discretion, and administrators use suspension as the primary means of corrective discipline when a student lands in their office.

The special education team at the school site are overwhelmed due to the increase in referrals for testing and the severe behaviors of the students. Many of the students they serve have come with behavior plans that do not seem to be working. The district-level special education program specialists are repeatedly called into the school to provide suggestions and supports. Unfortunately, they also express the same beliefs and sentiments as the teachers. One program specialist is overheard by a parent telling the special education teacher, "I am so glad my children go to another school." She also condones and recommends the suspensions and expulsions of special education students at this school, giving it the highest number of suspensions in the district.

Staff morale is low. Maintaining a positive school climate is of high importance at Wilbur School, but annual surveys to the community and quarterly surveys to staff are not reflecting this to be the case. For example, recent teacher input surveys revealed that less than 30 percent of teachers felt comfortable collaborating with their colleagues, only 20 percent felt supported by their administrators, and 80 percent felt unsafe on campus and in the surrounding community. Additionally, 80 percent of teachers reported dissatisfaction with how discipline was addressed. In addition, teachers have commented that PBIS and restorative justice practices "are not effective for the school." The staff have expressed concern regarding safety and have requested campus security and the addition of an alternative classroom or in-school suspension room option. Several teachers have also become vocal at district board meetings about the need for additional alternative education sites. In fact, one board member has made it her number-one priority to advocate for additional exclusionary sites.

The teachers' union representative for the school has also become vocal regarding the discipline and culture at this school. This has resulted in a school psychologist being on site extra days to help implement culturally responsive teaching. Although the school psychologist is on site more often, she is bombarded with calls to respond to student misbehavior and special education assessments, making it impossible to help with the preventive system or targeted and individualized interventions. In addition, there is no clear system for what culturally responsive teaching implementation should include, and no one is sufficiently trained on what best practices of implementation should look like. As a result, staff are confused about what they are doing with any of the behavior initiatives. Components of each are visible in a handful of classrooms, but overall there is no consistency or clarity, resulting in similar outcomes.

The principal of 20 years becomes so frustrated with what she calls "the lack of support from the district office" that she resigns in the middle of the school year, leaving the school with an interim administrator. The interim administrator attempts to train the school staff by bringing in a self-proclaimed expert on culturally responsive teaching from the district office. Although the teachers seem to be excited about the ideas and concepts presented to them, there is no clarity on the *how* and no follow-through after one staff training on the subject, resulting in a classic case of the behavior initiative implementation chasm.

Solutions Phase Step 1: The Five *Whys*

Now that you have read the scenario, we need first to identify the *whys* of implementation failure. When using this level of analysis, we've rarely approached this task in isolation. It is strongly encouraged that you dig deep to find the root causes with your guiding coalition, leadership team, and the like. When finding solutions, you need to know exactly what problem you are trying to solve. This process is best done with multiple participants who represent a diverse cross-section of your staff population (i.e., a representative from each grade level or department, a school psychologist, a school counselor, an intervention teacher, a curriculum coach, administration) and not just the principal alone.

The first step is to uncover the real reasons for your underlying problem. LeMahieu, Bryk, Gunrow, and Gomez (2017) call it "Asking the 'Why' Questions." Conzemius and O'Neill (2013) call it the "Five Whys Analysis." Whatever you want to call it, the process remains the same: If you probe several layers beneath the obvious symptoms of a problem, you will uncover the underlying deep causes leading you to a point of action.

To start, develop a problem statement acknowledging that a problem exists. Next, identify a potential cause of the problem. Then ask why that cause occurs. Follow up that response with another why question. Repeat this process five times, or until you get to the underlying cause of the problem. The *why* analysis will be your team's jumping-in point for identifying the problems and their potential causes.

Solutions Phase—Step 1: Five *Whys* Sample (based on the Wilbur School scenario)	
Five *Whys*	
Why 1: Why are the behavior initiatives not working at this school?	**Response:** A lot of students are not responding to them.
Why 2: Why are students not responding?	**Response:** They are unclear on the behavior expectations of the school.
Why 3: Why are they unclear on the behavior expectations of the school?	**Response:** We haven't identified our goals as a staff or been trained on the behavior initiatives we are trying to implement.
Why 4: Why haven't we identified our goals as a staff or been trained on the behavior initiatives we are trying to implement?	**Response:** We feel overwhelmed and that there is always some "next best thing" offered each year before figuring out why the current behavior initiatives are not working.
Why 5: Why do you feel overwhelmed and that a "next best thing" will be offered next year before figuring out why your current behavior initiatives are not working?	**Response:** We haven't spent time together identifying the social and emotional mission of our school or time to develop consistent implementation actions and proficiency measures.
Collective Commitment: Let's create time to define our social and emotional mission, check our beliefs, and develop clarity around the *why* and *how* of implementing these behavior initiatives together so that we are on the same page before we say it is not working.	

Note: Before you move on to Step 2 of the solutions phase, insert in the "Five Whys Summary Sheet" the problem statements and identified themes around the practice scenario based on your five *whys*.

Solutions Phase—Step 1: Five *Whys* Sample, continued

Five *Whys* Summary Sheet

Problem Statement (sample problem statements from the scenario):

1. Staff do not believe the students will respond to the behavior initiatives being implemented.

2. Staff do not have high expectations for students at the school.

3. Staff are overwhelmed with the amount of behavior challenges throughout the school.

4. There is lack of clarity around the mission and behavior initiatives implementation actions, resulting in confusion and inconsistency of implementation.

5. No training has been provided around the selected behavior initiatives for the school.

Identified Themes:

- Lack of beliefs and high expectations for students

- No behavioral system in place

- Inconsistency of implementation

- No identified purpose or goals around implementation

- No accountability or effectiveness measures

- Lack of proper training

- Sustainability plan is not in place

- Students are disciplined in an inconsistent manner by both staff and administration

- Staff feel students are not receiving consequences for negative behavior nor positive reinforcements for acceptable behavior

- Data show that suspensions have increased across all demographics with significant increases in suspensions among students of color, students of low socioeconomic status, and students with disabilities

Thoughts resonating with you so far:

_____

_____

_____

_____

_____

_____

Five *Whys*

Why 1:	**Response:**
Why 2:	**Response:**
Why 3:	**Response:**
Why 4:	**Response:**
Why 5:	**Response:**

Collective Commitment:

Five *Whys* Summary Sheet

Problem Statements:

1.

2.

3.

4.

5.

Identified Themes:

Solutions Phase Step 2: The Fishbone Process

For the team's examination of possible causes of why the problem exists, you will need a tool to help work through the process of identifying the problem and visually representing the product to focus on solutions for any particular cause. LeMahieu et al. (2017) call this tool a *fishbone diagram*. Conzemius and O'Neill (2013) call it a *cause-and-effect diagram*. Originally created by Japanese engineer Kaoru Ishikawa in 1943, it is also referred to as an *Ishikawa Diagram*.

We use this process with teams to help them unpack any variation of problems they are facing (i.e., addressing a problem with several complex aspects to it, addressing multiple problems, or addressing a problem that seems to be an outlier with no obvious cause). Once the problem has been identified and a concise statement has been created for it, you will identify major categories that are likely sources of the problem.

Examine every major category using the *why* process again until your team feels all possible sources have been exhausted for each major category. During a brainstorming session, you will draw columns on a whiteboard, using the major categories as headings, and have your team write a potential source of the problem on a sticky note and place it under the appropriate heading. Then repeat this process for each category. This visual will allow you to see categories that are more heavily represented than others and/or potential causes that repeat across the major categories.

Instructions for Using the Fishbone Diagram

The fishbone template provided in Figure 8.6 gives you an idea of how to create your own diagram. First, you'll create the "bones" or major lines for each category. Develop labels based on the aspects of the problem you have identified. Use broad/general terms for the header categories. Some examples are *master schedule, measurement, policies, professional development, equipment, students and families, people, standards, instruction, climate, procedures, processes, assessment, technology, curriculum, resources, facilities,* and *materials*. Draw smaller bones from each major bone for each category until all the ideas generated from the brainstorming session are listed on the diagram: The larger bones represent the major categories (the column headings), and the smaller bones are the suggested causes generated from the *whys* (the contents of the sticky notes). Figure 8.7 is a sample fishbone diagram based on the Wilbur School scenario.

Some causes have deeper layers that can use further unpacking. As mentioned earlier, this process could be used with a problem having several complex aspects to it or a problem that is addressing multiple issues. This would be a process to probe deeper. Use the *why* process again to create a new fishbone from a cause that has many factors that contribute to it.

For example, under the initial problem (effect) of "Implementation Failure/Poor Student Outcomes," the team created a major bone labeled "Leadership" (see Figure 8.7). From the major bone "Leadership," there is a cause labeled "no mission/vision established." That cause in itself has many factors that need unpacking. A new fishbone could be created as a new problem (effect) "no mission/vision established" with new major bones coming from it using the *why* process to brainstorm causes to identify factors potentially leading to that effect. This process will allow schools to get past the implementation chasm and identify why an initiative is struggling to gain momentum, rather than ditching it and running off to find "the next best thing."

Note: You already began the work of identifying possible common causes (bones) that affect behavior initiative implementation based on the Behavior Initiative Self-Assessment you used during Phase 2 of the SW-BIP. For example, based on the Wilbur School scenario, we used four categories from the self-assessment (leadership, funding, professional development, and accountability) and four additional categories from themes that emerged (students, community, special education, and district-level supports). You may find that other categories or general areas better fit into your fishbone as you delve deeper into this process (e.g., master schedule, measurement, policies, professional development).

FIGURE 8.6 ■ Fishbone Template

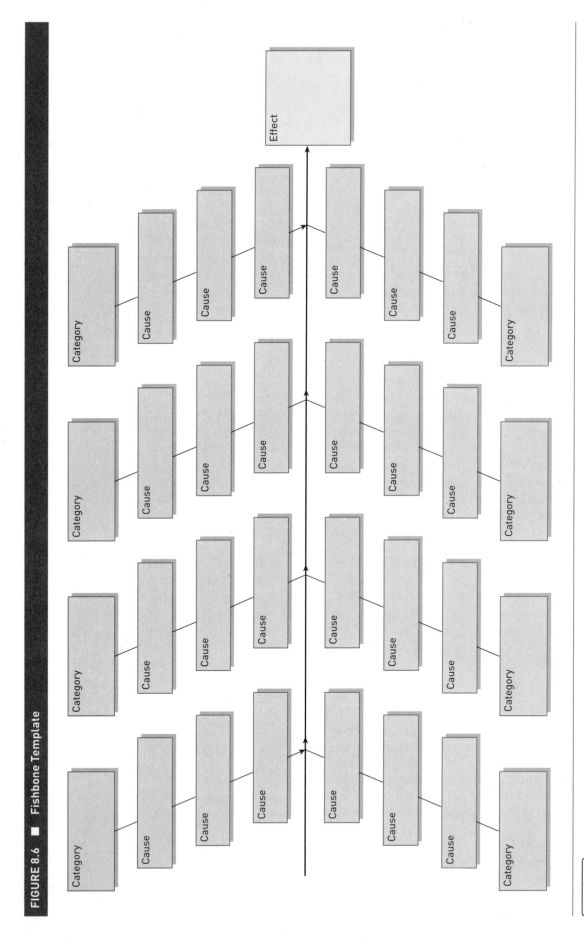

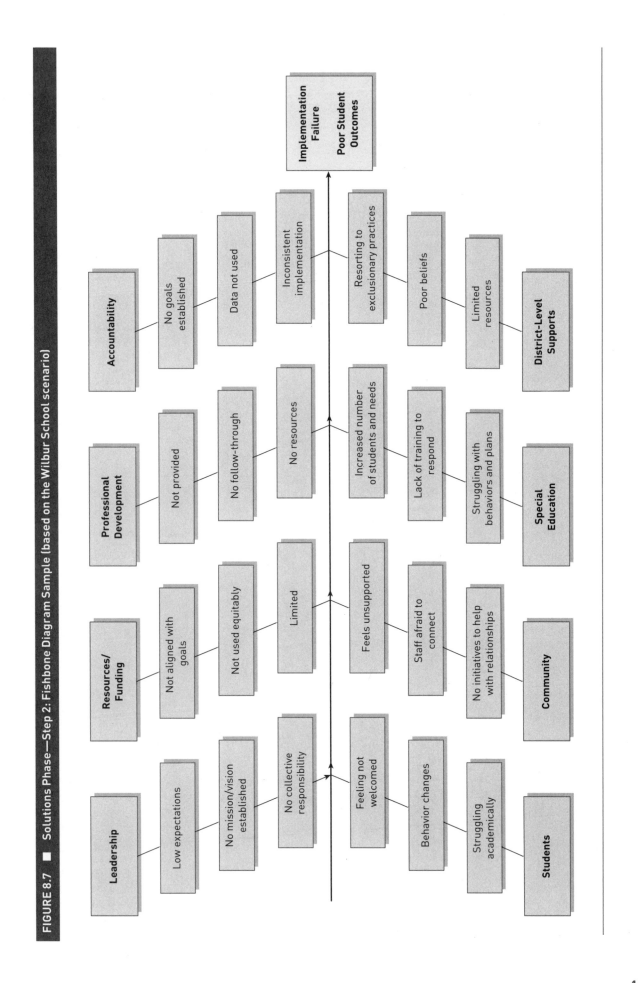

FIGURE 8.7 ■ Solutions Phase—Step 2: Fishbone Diagram Sample (based on the Wilbur School scenario)

Leadership
- Low expectations
- No mission/vision established
- No collective responsibility

Resources/Funding
- Not aligned with goals
- Not used equitably
- Limited

Professional Development
- Not provided
- No follow-through
- No resources

Accountability
- No goals established
- Data not used
- Inconsistent implementation

Students
- Struggling academically
- Behavior changes
- Feeling not welcomed

Community
- No initiatives to help with relationships
- Staff afraid to connect
- Feels unsupported

Special Education
- Struggling with behaviors and plans
- Lack of training to respond
- Increased number of students and needs

District-Level Supports
- Limited resources
- Poor beliefs
- Resorting to exclusionary practices

Implementation Failure

Poor Student Outcomes

Solutions Phase—Step 3: Action Plan

Solutions Phase—Step 3: Action Plan Sample (based on the Wilbur School scenario)

Behavior Initiative Action Plan: Schoolwide Version

Schoolwide Mission:

Wilbur School's mission is to support all students academically and social and emotionally at high levels in order to cultivate students who become productive and tolerant members of society.

What behavior initiative will be implemented? Culturally responsive teaching (CRT)

Behavior Initiative Implementation Objective(s):

- Establish a system to implement CRT schoolwide
- Improve school culture
- Establish relationships with students and the community
- Improve academic achievement
- Improve discipline

Long-Term Schoolwide SMART Goal:

Identified and taught CRT classroom best practices will be implemented in every classroom by the end of the next school year (2019–2020) as measured by improved school culture satisfaction surveys at multiple levels (teacher, parent, and student).

Baseline:

Currently at the middle of the school year (2018–2019), there is no observable evidence of CRT classroom best practices implemented in every classroom (0% implementation based on baseline classroom observations).

There are no identified or taught CRT classroom best practices expected in every classroom.

There is no evidence of student work demonstrating CRT best-practice implementation in every classroom.

School culture survey baseline data reveal 20% school culture satisfaction from teachers, 20% school culture satisfaction from parents, and 10% school culture satisfaction from students.

Long-Term Schoolwide SMART Goal Proficiency Measures:

By the end of the following school year (2019–2020), every classroom will have observable evidence of implementing the identified and taught CRT classroom best practices as measured by 100% of the classroom teachers demonstrating evidence of CRT implementation based on administrator classroom walk-throughs.

School culture satisfaction survey data will demonstrate 80% or higher satisfaction regarding school culture from teachers, parents, and students.

Quarterly SMART Goals

SMART GOAL	**SMART GOAL**	**SMART GOAL**	**SMART GOAL**
Quarter 1:	**Quarter 2:**	**Quarter 3:**	**Quarter 4:**
By the end of the 2018–2019 school year, the leadership team will have identified and provided adequate training on the CRT classroom best practices that can be implemented with observable evidence in every classroom.	By the beginning of the 2019–2020 school year, the leadership team will have provided a refresher training for the identified CRT classroom best practices that can be implemented with observable evidence in every classroom.	By the middle of the 2019–2020 school year, the leadership team will have provided an opportunity for input from CRT implementers on what is needed to continue best-practice implementation of CRT and provide additional supports, training, and resources based on student data.	By the end of the 2019–2020 school year, every classroom will have observable evidence of implementing the identified and taught CRT classroom best practices, and school culture satisfaction survey data will demonstrate 80% or higher satisfaction regarding school culture from teachers, parents, and students.

Quarterly SMART Goals (Continued)

Measure of proficiency:	**Measure of proficiency:**	**Measure of proficiency:**	**Measure of proficiency:**
. . . as measured by administrator walk-through data *and* quarterly submitted evidence of implementation from teachers to the leadership team.	. . . as measured by administrator walk-through data *and* quarterly submitted evidence of implementation from teachers to the leadership team *and* beginning of the 2019–2020 school year teacher, parent, and student school culture satisfaction surveys improved to 50% satisfaction from all levels.	. . . as measured by administrator walk-through data *and* quarterly submitted evidence of implementation from teachers to the leadership team.	. . . as measured by 100% of the classroom teachers demonstrating evidence of CRT implementation based on administrator classroom walk-throughs *and* quarterly submitted student work evidence of implementation to the leadership team *and* end of the 2019–2020 school year teacher, parent, and student school culture satisfaction survey results will have improved to 80% or higher satisfaction from all levels (teachers, parents, students).

Summary of SW-BIP: Self-Assessment, Five *Whys*, and Fishbone
Results to Actions

Self-Assessment Score:	**Five *Whys*—**list problem statement(s):	**Fishbone—**list bone categories (cause and effect):
<u>20/120 points</u> + Have a leadership team established to help with behavior initiative implementation — Do not have a mission for implementation Do not have proper training Do not have clear expectations and accountability measures for implementation	Staff are overwhelmed with the amount of behavior challenges throughout the school. There is lack of clarity around the mission and behavior initiative implementation actions, resulting in confusion and inconsistency of implementation. No training has been provided around the selected behavior initiatives for the school.	Leadership Resources/Funding Professional Development Accountability Students Community Special Education District-Level Supports

Priority Actions	By when	By whom	Action progress check (Are we on track? What are next steps and by when?)
Action 1: Message the mission around the selected behavior initiative implementation and identify leadership team roles based on expertise.	By the end of the 2018–2019 school year	By the leadership team	On track as measured by evidence of revised mission and roles/responsibilities identified for implementation by expertise.
Action 2: Educate teachers and community on the established long-term and short-term SMART goals using data.	Ongoing By the beginning of the 2019–2020 school year, at least two methods of sharing SMART goals and priority actions with teachers and the community	By the leadership team	In progress. All teachers were provided with an overview of the SMART goals during the back-to-school all-staff workshop. Currently planning the community workshops around the SMART goals, to be completed and delivered by September 2019.
Action 3: Identify and schedule ongoing trainings based on needs of the teachers so that every teacher will be adequately taught how to implement the CRT classroom best practices expected to be observed in every classroom.	Ongoing By the beginning of the 2019–2020 school year, at least one training delivered to all teachers	By the hired CRT expert training in collaboration with the leadership team	In progress. Currently in the teacher stakeholder training needs-assessment stage. Data collection to be completed by September 2019.

Behavior Initiative Action Plan: Schoolwide Version

Schoolwide Mission:

What behavior initiative will be implemented?

Behavior Initiative Implementation Objective(s):

Long-Term Schoolwide SMART Goal:

Baseline:

Long-Term Schoolwide SMART Goal Proficiency Measures:

Quarterly SMART Goals

SMART GOAL Quarter 1:	SMART GOAL Quarter 2:	SMART GOAL Quarter 3:	SMART GOAL Quarter 4:
Measure of proficiency:	Measure of proficiency:	Measure of proficiency:	Measure of proficiency:

Behavior Initiative Action Plan: Schoolwide Version

Summary of SW-BIP: Self-Assessment, Five *Whys*, and Fishbone

Results to Actions

Self-Assessment Score: _____ + −	Five *Whys*—list problem statement(s): _____ _____ _____ _____ _____ _____	Fishbone—list bone categories (cause and effect): _____ _____ _____ _____ _____ _____ _____

Priority Actions	By when	By whom	Action progress check (Are we on track? What are next steps and by when?)
Action 1			
Action 2			
Action 3			

online resources ▶ Available for download at **http://resources.corwin.com/BuildingBehavior**

Behavior Initiative Action Plan: Districtwide Version

Districtwide Mission:

What behavior initiative will be implemented?

Behavior Initiative Implementation Objective(s):

Long-Term Districtwide SMART Goal:

Baseline:

Long-Term Districtwide SMART Goal Proficiency Measures:

Quarterly SMART Goals

SMART GOAL Quarter 1:	**SMART GOAL** Quarter 2:	**SMART GOAL** Quarter 3:	**SMART GOAL** Quarter 4:
Measure of proficiency:	**Measure of proficiency:**	**Measure of proficiency:**	**Measure of proficiency:**

Behavior Initiative Action Plan: Districtwide Version
Summary of DW-BIP: Self-Assessment, Five *Whys*, and Fishbone Results to Actions

| Self-Assessment Score: _____

 +

 – | Five *Whys*—list problem statement(s):

 _____
 _____
 _____
 _____
 _____
 _____ | Fishbone—list bone categories (cause and effect):

 _____
 _____
 _____
 _____
 _____
 _____
 _____ |

Priority Actions	By when	By whom	Action progress check (Are we on track? What are next steps and by when?)
Action 1			
Action 2			
Action 3			

online resources ↘ Available for download at **http://resources.corwin.com/BuildingBehavior**

SECTION 3: CLOSING THOUGHTS: TIPS AND SUGGESTIONS FROM THE AUTHORS

I alone cannot change the world, but I can cast a stone across the waters to create many ripples.

—*Mother Teresa*

ALWAYS BASE YOUR DECISIONS AND ACTIONS ON *WHAT IS BEST FOR ALL STUDENTS*

Have a moral compass

Be prepared to educate naysayers on the reasons for implementation

Model what you preach

Be relentless

Have courage to do what is right

Be willing to think outside the box

Use data to make decisions

Make your behavior initiatives as high a priority as your academic initiatives

Build collective agreement and responsibility around implementation

Take the time to educate your stakeholders

Believe in the work: Always remember your WHY

Hold high expectations for students and staff

Understand the why and best practices around the behavior initiative you decide to implement

Have difficult discussions

Face difficult situations

Implement it in a systematic way

Be aware of the implementation chasm

Use the SchoolWide or DistrictWide Behavior Initiatives Process (SW-BIP or DW-BIP) design for effective implementation

Take the time to learn, train, implement, and monitor best-practice implementation

Align your long-term and quarterly SMART goals around implementation with high-priority actions

Invest in proper ongoing training and development based on the needs of your students

We began this work in order to understand the problem that schools and districts are facing and to help them identify the best behavior initiatives based on their needs as well as to understand why some schools move from one initiative to another so quickly. We defined the most common behavior initiatives implemented worldwide and provided the knowledge, tools, and best-practice resources needed to help your school or district move past the implementation chasm and begin the work of building effective behavior initiatives in your school or district. We explained the *why* behind each initiative and helped you self-assess your implementation status and needs, guiding you through beginning the work of building an action plan for implementation to prevent or overcome the behavior initiative implementation chasm. We provided you with a list of best-practice resources to help ensure training and ongoing professional development are being provided for all stakeholders. This book is not designed to replace formal training on any of the initiatives but, rather, to help you make an informed decision about the needs of your school and build and implement an action plan with effective results for your students.

Now it is time for the difficult but meaningful work for your students. To reiterate our charge from Part I of this book, with regard to whichever behavior initiative(s) your school may currently be using, it's not that *it* isn't working; it's the *implementation of it* that isn't working. Mistakes are inevitable. The SW-BIP will help you identify why and where they happened and how to correct them. Don't let the implementation chasm prevent your initiative from getting off the ground. Use this process to build and implement best-practice behavior initiatives in a systemic and sustainable manner and get these practices rooted deeply into the culture of your school. Your students are depending on you.

REFERENCES

Aceves, T. C., & Orosco, M. J. (2014). Culturally responsive teaching (Document No. IC-2). Retrieved from University of Florida, Collaboration for Effective Educator, Development, Accountability, and Reform Center, http://ceedar.education.ufl.edu/tools/innovation-configurations/

Anderson, C., Barnes, M. S., Beane, C., Bishop, J., Davis, E., Fishkind, P., & Truman, S. (2014). *Restorative practices: Fostering healthy relationships & promoting positive discipline in schools: A guide for educators*. Washington, DC: Advancement Project.

Anderson, E. M., Blitz, L. V., & Saastamoinen, M. (2015). Exploring a school-university model for professional development with classroom staff: Teaching trauma-informed approaches. *School Community Journal, 25*(2), 113–134.

Annette, J. (2005). Character, civic renewal and service learning for democratic citizenship in higher education. *British Journal of Educational Studies, 53*(3), 326–340.

Ashley, J., & Burke, K. (2009). Implementing restorative justice: A guide for schools. *Illinois Criminal Justice Information Authority, 24.*

Balfanz, R., & Boccanfuso, C. (2007). *Falling off the path to graduation: Early indicators brief*. Baltimore, MD: Everyone Graduates Center.

Battistich, V. (2011). *Character education, prevention, and positive youth development*. Washington, DC: Character Education Partnership.

Bazemore, G., & Stinchcomb, J. (2004). A civic engagement model of reentry: Involving community through service and restorative justice. *Federal Probation, 68,* 14.

Bazemore, G., & Umbreit, M. (2001). A comparison of four restorative justice models. *OJJDP Juvenile Justice Bulletin*. Retrieved from https://www.ncjrs.gov/pdffiles1/ojjdp/184738.pdf

Benazzi, L., Horner, R. H., & Good, R. H. (2006). Effects of behavior support team composition on the technical adequacy and contextual fit of behavior support plans. *The Journal of Special Education, 40*(3), 160–170.

Benner, G. J., Nelson, J. R., Sanders, E. A., & Ralston, N. C. (2012). Behavior intervention for students with externalizing behavior problems: Primary-level standard protocol. *Exceptional Children, 78*(2), 181–198.

Benninga, J. S., Berkowitz, M. W., Kuehn, P., & Smith, K. (2003). The relationship of character education implementation and academic achievement in elementary schools. *Journal of Research in Character Education, 1*(1), 19–32.

Berkowitz, M. W., Althof, W., & Bier, M. C. (2012). The practice of pro-social education. In P. Brown, M. Corrigan, & A. Higgins-D'Alessandro (Eds.), *The handbook of prosocial education* (Vol. 1, pp. 71–90). Lanham MD: Rowman & Littlefield.

Berkowitz, M. W., & Bier, M. C. (2004). Research-based character education. *The ANNALS of the American Academy of Political and Social Science, 591*(1), 72–85.

Berkowitz, M. W., Bier, M. C., & McCauley, B. (2017). Towards a science of character education: Frameworks for identifying and implementing effective practices. *Journal of Character Education, 13*(1), 33–51.

Blood, P. (2005, August). *The Australian context–restorative practices as a platform for cultural change in schools*. Paper presented at the XIV World Congress of Criminology, Philadelphia, Pennsylvania.

Blood, P., & Thorsborne, M. (2005, March). *The challenge of culture change: Embedding restorative practice in schools*. Paper presented at the 6th International Conference on Conferencing, Circles and other Restorative Practices, 'Building a Global Alliance for Restorative Practices and Family Empowerment', Sydney, Australia.

Blood, P., & Thorsborne, M. (2006, October). *Overcoming resistance to whole-school uptake of restorative practices*. Paper presented at the International Institute of Restorative Practice's 'The Next Step: Developing Restorative Communities, Part 2' Conference, Bethlehem, Pennsylvania.

Bloom, S. L., & Sreedhar, S. Y. (2008). The sanctuary model of trauma-informed organizational change. *Reclaiming Children and Youth, 17*(3), 48.

Borba, M. (2002). *Building moral intelligence: The seven essential virtues that teach kids to do the right thing*. New York: Wiley.

Boston, B. O., Pearson, S. S., & Halperin, S. (2005). *Restoring the balance between academics and civic engagement in public schools*. Washington, DC: American Youth Policy Forum and Association for Supervision and Curriculum Development.

Bradshaw, C. P., Koth, C. W., Bevans, K. B., Ialongo, N., & Leaf, P. J. (2008). The impact of school-wide positive behavioral interventions and supports (PBIS) on the organizational health of elementary schools. *School Psychology Quarterly, 23*(4), 462–473.

Bradshaw, C. P., Koth, C. W., Thornton, L. A., & Leaf, P. J. (2009). Altering school climate through school-wide positive behavioral interventions and supports: Findings from a group-randomized effectiveness trial. *Prevention Science, 10*(2), 100–115.

Bradshaw, C. P., Pas, E. T., Goldweber, A., Rosenberg, M. S., & Leaf, P. J. (2012). Integrating school-wide positive behavioral interventions and supports with tier 2 coaching to student support teams: The PBIS plus model. *Advances in School Mental Health Promotion, 5*(3), 177–193.

Bradshaw, C. P., Reinke, W. M., Brown, L. D., Bevans, K. B., & Leaf, P. J. (2008). Implementation of school-wide positive behavioral interventions and supports (PBIS) in elementary schools: Observations from a randomized trial. *Education and Treatment of Children, 31*(1), 1–26.

Bradshaw, C. P., Waasdorp, T. E., & Leaf, P. J. (2012). Effects of school-wide positive behavioral interventions and supports on child behavior problems. *Pediatrics, 130*(5), e1136–e1145.

Brown-Jeffy, S., & Cooper, J. (2011). Toward a conceptual framework of culturally relevant pedagogy: An overview of the conceptual and theoretical literature. *Teacher Education Quarterly, 38*(1), 65–84. Retrieved from http://www.jstor.org/stable/23479642

Bryk, A. S., Gomez, L. M., Grunow, A., & LeMahieu, P. G. (2015). *Learning to improve: How America's schools can get better at getting better.* Cambridge, MA: Harvard Education Press.

Bulach, C. R. (2002). Implementing a character education curriculum and assessing its impact on student behavior. *The Clearing House, 76*(2), 79–83.

Burke, M. D., Hagan-Burke, S., & Sugai, G. (2003). The efficacy of function- based interventions for students with learning disabilities who exhibit escape-maintained problem behaviors: Preliminary results from a single-case experiment. *Learning Disability Quarterly, 26*(1), 15–25.

Cameron, L., & Thorsborne, M. (2001). Restorative justice and school discipline: Mutually exclusive? In H. Strang & J. Braithwaite (Eds.), *Restorative justice and civil society* (pp. 180–194). Cambridge, UK: Cambridge University Press.

Carr, E. G., Horner, R. H., Turnbull, A. P., Marquis, J. G., McLaughlin, D. M., McAtee, M. L., . . . Doolabh, A. (1999). *Positive behavior support for people with developmental disabilities: A research synthesis* (D. Braddock, Ed.). Washington, DC: American Association on Mental Retardation.

Chafouleas, S. M., Johnson, A. H., Overstreet, S., & Santos, N. M. (2016). Toward a blueprint for trauma-informed service delivery in schools. *School Mental Health, 8*(1), 144–162.

Claassen, R., & Claassen, R. (2008). *Discipline that restores: Strategies to create respect, cooperation, and responsibility in the classroom.* Charleston, SC: Ron and Roxanne Claassen.

Cohen, J. A., Mannarino, A. P., & Deblinger, E. (2016). *Treating trauma and traumatic grief in children and adolescents.* Guilford Publications.

Cohen, J., McCabe, L., Michelli, N. M., & Pickeral, T. (2009). School climate: Research, policy, practice, and teacher education. *Teachers College Record, 111*(1), 180–213.

Colvin, G., & Sugai, G. (2018). *Seven steps for developing a proactive schoolwide discipline plan: A guide for principals and leadership teams,* 2nd ed. Thousand Oaks, CA: Corwin.

Conzemius, A. E., & O'Neill, J. (2013). *The handbook for SMART school teams: Revitalizing best practices for collaboration.* Bloomington, IN: Solution Tree Press.

Cook, B. G., Landrum, T. J., Tankersley, M., & Kauffman, J. M. (2003). Bringing research to bear on practice: Effecting evidence-based instruction for students with emotional or behavioral disorders. *Education and Treatment of Children, 26*(4), 345–361.

Copeland, W. E., Keeler, G., Angold, A., & Costello, E. J. (2007). Traumatic events and posttraumatic stress in childhood. *Archives of General Psychiatry, 64*(5), 577–584.

Craig, S. E. (2015). *Trauma-sensitive schools.* New York: Teachers College Press.

Crone, D. A., Hawken, L. S., & Horner, R. H. (2010). *Responding to problem behavior in schools: The behavior education program,* 2nd ed. New York: Guilford.

Cutrone, J., & Director, A. E. (2009). *Final report of the Go To 2040 crime and Justice Planning Initiative.* Chicago, IL: Illinois Criminal Justice Information Authority.

Domitrovich, C. E., Durlak, J. A., Staley, K. C., & Weissberg, R. P. (2017). Social-emotional competence: An essential factor for promoting positive adjustment and reducing risk in school children. *Child Development, 88*(2), 408–416.

Dorado, J. S., Martinez, M., McArthur, L. E., & Leibovitz, T. (2016). Healthy Environments and Response to Trauma in Schools (HEARTS): A whole-school, multi-level, prevention and intervention program for creating trauma-informed, safe and supportive schools. *School Mental Health, 8*(1), 163–176.

DuFour, R., & Reeves, D. (2016). The futility of PLC lite. *Phi Delta Kappan, 97*(6), 69–71.

Durlak, J. A., Domitrovich, C. E., Weissberg, R. P., & Gullotta, T. P. (Eds.). (2015). *Handbook of social and emotional learning: Research and practice.* New York: Guilford.

Durlak, J. A., Weissberg, R. P., & Pachan, M. (2010). A meta-analysis of after-school programs that seek to promote personal and social skills in children and adolescents. *American Journal of Community Psychology, 45*(3–4), 294–309.

Durlak, J. A., Weissberg, R. P., Dymnicki, A. B., Taylor, R. D., & Schellinger, K. B. (2011). The impact of enhancing students' social and emotional learning: A meta-analysis of school-based universal interventions. *Child Development, 82*(1), 405–432.

Epstein, M. H., & Walker, H. M. (2002). Special education: Best practices and First Step to Success. In B. J. Burns & K. Hoagwood (Eds.), *Community treatment for youth:*

Evidence-based interventions for severe emotional and behavioral disorders (pp. 179–197). New York: Oxford University Press.

Fairbanks, S., Sugai, G., Guardino, D., & Lathrop, M. (2007). Response to intervention: Examining classroom behavior support in second grade. *Exceptional Children, 73*(3), 288–310.

Felitti, V. J., Anda, R. F., Nordenberg, D., Williamson, D. F., Spitz, A. M., Edwards, V., Koss, M. P., & Marks, J. S. (1998). Relationship of childhood abuse and household dysfunction to many of the leading causes of death in adults. The Adverse Childhood Experiences (ACE) Study. *American Journal of Preventive Medicine, 14*(4), 245–258.

Filter, K. J., McKenna, M. K., Benedict, E. A., Horner, R. H., Todd, A., & Watson, J. (2007). Check in/check out: A post-hoc evaluation of an efficient, secondary-level targeted intervention for reducing problem behaviors in schools. *Education and Treatment of Children, 30*(1), 69–84.

Flinspach, S. L. (2001). Strengthening civic education: Three strategies for school officials. *Popular Government, 66*, 31–38.

Frey, N., Fisher, D., & Smith, D. (2019). *All learning is social and emotional: Helping students develop essential skills for the classroom and beyond.* Alexandria, VA: ASCD.

Friedlaender, D., Burns, D., Lewis-Charp, H., Cook-Harvey, C. M., & Darling-Hammond, L. (2014). Student-centered schools: Closing the opportunity gap (SCOPE Research Brief). Retrieved from Stanford Center for Opportunity Policy in Education website: https://edpolicy.stanford.edu/sites/default/files/scope-pub-student-centered-research-brief.pdf.

Fronius, T., Persson, H., Guckenburg, S., Hurley, N., & Petrosino, A. (2016). *Restorative justice in US schools: A research review.* San Francisco, CA: WestEd Justice and Prevention Training Center.

Gay, G. (2010). *Culturally responsive teaching: Theory, research, and practice*, 2nd edition. New York: Teachers College Press.

Gest, S. D., & Gest, J. M. (2005). Reading tutoring for students at academic and behavioral risk: Effects on time-on-task in the classroom. *Education and Treatment of Children, 28*(1), 25–47.

Golly, A., Sprague, J., Walker, H., Beard, K., & Gorham, G. (2000). The first step to success program: An analysis of outcomes with identical twins across multiple baselines. *Behavioral Disorders, 25*(3), 170–182.

Gray, S., & Drewery, W. (2011). Restorative practices meet key competencies: Class meetings as pedagogy. *International Journal on School Disaffection, 8*(1), 13–21.

Greenberg, M. T., Weissberg, R. P., O'brien, M. U., Zins, J. E., Fredericks, L., Resnik, H., & Elias, M. J. (2003). Enhancing school-based prevention and youth development through coordinated social, emotional, and academic learning. *American Psychologist, 58*(6–7), 466.

Greene, R. W. (2009). *Lost at school: Why our kids with behavioral challenges are falling through the cracks and how we can help them.* New York: Simon & Schuster.

Gurwitch, R. H., Messer, E. P., Masse, J., Olafson, E., Boat, B. W., & Putnam, F. W. (2016). Child–Adult Relationship Enhancement (CARE): An evidence-informed program for children with a history of trauma and other behavioral challenges. *Child Abuse & Neglect, 53*, 138–145.

Hammond, Z. L. (2014). *Culturally responsive teaching and the brain: Promoting authentic engagement and rigor among culturally and linguistically diverse students.* Thousand Oaks, CA: Corwin.

Hannigan, J., & Hannigan, J. (2016). Comparison of traditional and innovative discipline beliefs in administrators. *CLEARvoz Journal, 3*(1).

Hannigan, J. D., & Hannigan, J. E. (2017). *Don't suspend me! An alternative discipline toolkit.* Thousand Oaks, CA: Corwin.

Hannigan, J. D., & Hannigan, J. (2018a). *The PBIS tier two handbook: A practical approach to implementing the champion model.* Thousand Oaks, CA: Corwin.

Hannigan, J. D., & Hannigan, J. (2018b). *The PBIS tier three handbook: A practical approach to implementing the champion model.* Thousand Oaks, CA: Corwin.

Hannigan, J. D., & Hauser, L. (2015). *The PBIS tier one handbook: A practical approach to implementing the champion model.* Thousand Oaks, CA: Corwin.

Hansen, T. (2005). *Center for restorative justice & peacemaking.* St. Paul, MN: University of Minnesota.

Harrington, N. G., Giles, S. M., Hoyle, R. H., Feeney, G. J., & Yungbluth, S. C. (2001). Evaluation of the all stars character education and problem behavior prevention program: Effects on mediator and outcome variables for middle school students. *Health Education & Behavior, 28*(5), 533–546.

Harris, M. E., & Fallot, R. D. (2001). *Using trauma theory to design service systems.* San Francisco, CA: Jossey-Bass.

Harvey, M. T., Lewis-Palmer, T., Horner, R. H., & Sugai, G. (2003). Trans-situational interventions: Generalization of behavior support across school and home environments. *Behavioral Disorders, 28*(3), 299–312.

Hattie, J. (2009). *Visible learning.* New York: Routledge.

Hattie, J. (2018, October). *Visible Learning* plus *250+ influences on student achievement.* Retrieved from https://us.corwin.com/sites/default/files/250_influences_10.1.2018.pdf

Hopkins, B. (2002). Restorative justice in schools. *Support for Learning, 17*(3), 144–149.

Horner, R. H., Sugai, G., & Lewis, T. (2007). *Is school-wide positive behavior support an evidence-based practice.* Retrieved January 10, 2009 from http://www.apbs.org/files/101007evidencebase4pbs.pdf.

Horner, R. H., Sugai, G., Smolkowski, K., Eber, L., Nakasato, J., Todd, A. W., & Esperanza, J. (2009). A randomized, wait-list controlled effectiveness trial assessing school-wide positive behavior support in elementary schools. *Journal of Positive Behavior Interventions, 11*(3), 133–144.

Howard, G. (2016). *We can't teach what we don't know: White teachers, multiracial schools.* New York: Teachers College Press.

Howard, G. R. (2007). As diversity grows, so must we. *Educational Leadership, 64*(6), 16.

Iovannone, R., Greenbaum, P. E., Wang, W., Kincaid, D., Dunlap, G., & Strain, P. (2009). Randomized Controlled Trial of the Prevent—Teach—Reinforce (PTR) Tertiary intervention for students with problem behaviors: Preliminary outcomes. *Journal of Emotional and Behavioral Disorders, 17*(4), 213–225.

Irvin, L. K., Tobin, T. J., Sprague, J. R., Sugai, G., & Vincent, C. G. (2004). Validity of office discipline referral measures as indices of school-wide behavioral status and effects of school-wide behavioral interventions. *Journal of Positive Behavior Interventions, 6*(3), 131–147.

Jaycox, L. H., Langley, A. K., & Dean, K. L. (2009). *Support for Students Exposed to Trauma: The SSET program.* Santa Monica, CA: RAND Corporation.

Jaycox, L. H., Langley, A. K., & Hoover, S. A. (2018). *Cognitive Behavioral Intervention for Trauma in Schools (CBITS).* Santa Monica, CA: RAND Corporation.

Jaycox, L., Morse, L. K., & Tanielian, T. (2006). *How schools can help students recover from traumatic experiences: A toolkit for supporting long-term recovery.* Santa Monica, CA: Rand Corporation.

Jones, S. M., Bouffard, S. M., & Weissbourd, R. (2013). Educators' social and emotional skills vital to learning. *Phi Delta Kappan, 94*(8), 62–65.

Jones, S., Brush, K., Bailey, R., Brion-Meisels, G., McIntyre, J., Kahn, J., . . . Stickle, L. (2017). *Navigating SEL from the inside out.* Retrieved from https://www.wallacefoundation.org/knowledge-center/Documents/Navigating-Social-and-Emotional-Learning-from-the-Inside-Out.pdf

Karp, D. R., & Breslin, B. (2001). Restorative justice in school communities. *Youth & Society, 33*(2), 249–272.

Kecskemeti, M. (2013). A discursive approach to restorative practice: Improving the learning environment through professional learning. *Engage: The International Journal of Research and Practice on Student Engagement, 1*(1), 24–35.

Knight, J. (2018). *The impact cycle: What instructional coaches should do to foster powerful improvements in teaching.* Thousand Oaks, CA: Corwin.

Korpershoek, H., Harms, T., de Boer, H., van Kuijk, M., & Doolaard, S. (2016). A meta-analysis of the effects of classroom management strategies and classroom management programs on students' academic, behavioral, emotional, and motivational outcomes. *Review of Educational Research, 86*(3), 643–680.

Ladson-Billings, G. (1994). *The Dreamkeepers: Successful teachers of African-American students.* San Francisco, CA: Jossey-Bass.

Ladson-Billings, G. (1995a). But that's just good teaching! The case for culturally relevant pedagogy. *Theory into Practice, 34*(3), 159–165.

Ladson-Billings, G. (1995b). Toward a theory of culturally relevant pedagogy. *American Educational Research Journal, 32*(3), 465–491.

Lane, K. L., Wehby, J., Menzies, H. M., Doukas, G. L., Munton, S. M., & Gregg, R. M. (2003). Social skills instruction for students at risk for antisocial behavior: The effects of small-group instruction. *Behavioral Disorders, 28*(3), 229–248.

LeMahieu, P. G., Bryk, A. S., Grunow, A., & Gomez, L. M. (2017). Working to improve: Seven approaches to improvement science in education. *Quality Assurance in Education, 25*(1), 2–4.

Leming, J. S. (1997). Whither goes character education? Objectives, pedagogy, and research in education programs. *Journal of Education, 179*(2), 11–34.

Lickona, T., Schaps, E., & Lewis, C. (2002). *Eleven principles of effective character education. Special Topics, General. 50.* Retrieved from https://digitalcommons.unomaha.edu/slcestgen/50

Lickona, T., Schaps, E., & Lewis, C. (2007). *CEP's Eleven principles of effective character education.* Washington, DC: Character Education Partnership.

Litt, E. (1963). Civic education, community norms, and political indoctrination. *American Sociological Review, 28*, 69–75.

Losen, D. J. (2011). *Discipline policies, successful schools, and racial justice.* Boulder, CO: National Education Policy Center. Retrieved from http://nepc.colorado.edu/publication/discipline-policies

Mayer, G. (1995). Preventing antisocial behavior in the schools. *Journal of Applied Behavior Analysis, 28*, 467–478.

McDaniel, S. C., Houchins, D. E., & Robinson, C. (2016). The effects of check, connect, and expect on behavioral and academic growth. *Journal of Emotional and Behavioral Disorders, 24*(1), 42–53.

McInerney, M., & McKlindon, A. (2014). *Unlocking the door to learning: Trauma-informed classrooms & transformational schools.* Retrieved from https://www.elc-pa.org/wp-content/uploads/2015/06/Trauma-Informed-in-Schools-Classrooms-FINAL-December2014-2.pdf

McIntosh, K., Borgmeier, C., Anderson, C. M., Horner, R. H., Rodriguez, B. J., & Tobin, T. J. (2008). Technical adequacy of the Functional Assessment Checklist: Teachers and Staff (FACTS) FBA interview measure. *Journal of Positive Behavior Interventions, 10*(1), 33–45.

Milson, A. J., & Mehlig, L. M. (2002). Elementary school teachers' sense of efficacy for character education. *The Journal of Educational Research, 96*(1), 47–53.

Moore, G. A. (1991). Crossing the chasm: Marketing and selling high-tech products to mainstream customers. New York: Harper Business.

Morrison, B., Blood, P., & Thorsborne, M. (2005). Practicing restorative justice in school communities: Addressing the challenge of culture change. *Public Organization Review, 5*(4), 335–357.

National Alliance on Mental Illness. (n.d.). *Anxiety disorders.* Retrieved from https://www.nami.org/Learn-More/Mental-Health-Conditions/Anxiety-Disorders

O'Connell, T., Wachtel, B., & Wachtel, T. (1999). *Conferencing handbook: The new real justice training manual.* Pipersville, PA: Piper's Press.

O'Conner, R., De Feyter, J., Carr, A., Luo, J. L., & Romm, H. (2017). *A review of the literature on social and emotional learning for students ages 3–8: Characteristics of effective social and emotional learning programs (Part 1 of 4)* (REL 2017-245). Washington, DC: Regional Educational Laboratory Mid-Atlantic.

Osher, D., Kidron, Y., Brackett, M., Dymnicki, A., Jones, S., & Weissberg, R. P. (2016). Advancing the science and practice of social and emotional learning: Looking back and moving forward. *Review of Research in Education, 40*(1), 644–681.

Overstreet, S., & Chafouleas, S. M. (2016). Trauma-informed schools: Introduction to the special issue. *School Mental Health, 8,* 1–6.

Payne, L. D., Marks, L. J., & Bogan, B. L. (2007). Using curriculum-based assessment to address the academic and behavioral deficits of students with emotional and behavioral disorders. *Beyond Behavior, 16*(3), 3–6.

Payne, A. A., & Welch, K. (2015). Restorative justice in schools: The influence of race on restorative discipline. *Youth & Society, 47*(4), 539–564.

Person, A. E., Moiduddin, E., Hague-Angus, M., & Malone, L. M. (2009). *Survey of outcomes measurement in research on character education programs* (NCEE 2009-006). Washington, DC: National Center for Education Evaluation and Regional Assistance.

Reimer, K. (2011). An exploration of the implementation of restorative justice in an Ontario public school. *Canadian Journal of Educational Administration and Policy, 119.*

Restorative Justice Colorado. (2014, September 19). *Restorative justice practices definitions and models.* Retrieved from https://www.rjcolorado.org/_literature_153912/RJ_Models_Definitions

Restorative Schools Visions Project (RSVP). (2017). *Building restorative justice practitioner consensus for better student health* (Grant Number 20142280). Retrieved from http://restorativeschoolsproject.org/wp-content/uploads/2014/12/RSVP-Final-Report-August-2017.pdf

Revell, L., & Arthur, J. (2007). Character education in schools and the education of teachers. *Journal of Moral Education, 36*(1), 79–92.

Richter, M. M. (2006). *The relationship between principal leadership skills and school-wide positive behavior support: An exploratory study* (Doctoral dissertation). University of Missouri, Columbia.

Riley, E. (2017, March 17). *Implementing restorative practices in the classroom.* Retrieved from https://www.gettingsmart.com/2017/03/implementing-restorative-practices-in-the-classroom/

Rogers, E. M. (1962). *The diffusion of innovation.* New York: Free Press.

Romero, V. E., & Robertson, R. (2018). *Building resilience in students impacted by adverse childhood experiences: A whole-staff approach.* Thousand Oaks, CA: Corwin.

Ross, S. W., Romer, N., & Horner, R. H. (2012). Teacher well-being and the implementation of school-wide positive behavior interventions and supports. *Journal of Positive Behavior Interventions, 14*(2), 118–128.

Schiff, M. (2013). *Dignity, disparity and desistance: Effective restorative justice strategies to plug the "school-to-prison pipeline."* Paper presented at the Closing the School Discipline Gap: Research to Practice conference, Washington, DC.

Scott, T. M., Liaupsin, C., Nelson, C. M., & McIntyre, J. (2005). Team-based functional behavior assessment as a proactive public school process: A descriptive analysis of current barriers. *Journal of Behavioral Education, 14*(1), 57–71.

Scott, T. M., McIntyre, J., Liaupsin, C., Nelson, C. M., Conroy, M., & Payne, L. D. (2005). An examination of the relation between functional behavior assessment and selected intervention strategies with school-based teams. *Journal of Positive Behavior Interventions, 7*(4), 205–215.

Shumer, R., Lam, C., & Laabs, B. (2012). Ensuring good character and civic education: Connecting through service learning. *Asia Pacific Journal of Education, 32*(4), 430–440.

Simonsen, B., Myers, D., & Briere, D. E., III (2011). Comparing a behavioral Check-In/Check-Out (CICO) intervention to standard practice in an urban middle school setting using an experimental group design. *Journal of Positive Behavior Interventions, 13*(1), 31–48.

Skiba, R., & Peterson, R. (1999). The dark side of zero tolerance: Can punishment lead to safe schools? *Phi Delta Kappan, 80*(5), 372–382.

Skiba, R., & Rausch, M. K. (2006). School disciplinary systems: Alternatives to suspension and expulsion. In G. G. Bear & K. M. Minke (Eds.), *Children's needs III: Development, prevention, and intervention* (pp. 87–102). Washington, DC: National Association of School Psychologists.

Skowyra, K. R., & Cocozza, J. J. (2007). *Blueprint for change: A comprehensive model for the identification and treatment of youth with mental health needs in contact with the juvenile justice system.* Delmar, NY: Policy Research Associates.

Smith, D., Fisher, D., & Frey, N. (2015). *Better than carrots or sticks: Restorative practices for positive classroom management.* Alexandria, VA: ASCD.

Souers, K., with Hall, P. (2016). *Fostering resilient learners: Strategies for creating a trauma-sensitive classroom.* Alexandria, VA: ASCD.

Sprague, J., Walker, H., Golly, A., White, K., Myers, D. R., & Shannon, T. (2001). Translating research into effective practice: The effects of a universal staff and student intervention on indicators of discipline and school safety. *Education and Treatment of Children, 24,* 495–511.

Sprick, R. (2018). *Safe & Civil Schools series overview.* Retrieved from http://www.safeandcivilschools.com/products/scs_overview.php

Stinchcomb, J. B., Bazemore, G., & Riestenberg, N. (2006). Beyond zero tolerance: Restoring justice in secondary schools. *Youth Violence and Juvenile Justice, 4*(2), 123–147.

Substance Abuse and Mental Health Services Administration (SAMHSA). (n.d.). *Trauma-informed approach and trauma-specific interventions.* Retrieved from https://www.samhsa.gov/nctic/trauma-interventions

Sugai, G., & Horner, R. H. (2010). School-wide positive behavior support: Establishing a continuum of evidence based practices. *Journal of Evidence-Based Practices for Schools, 11*(1), 62–83.

Todd, A. W., Campbell, A. L., Meyer, G. G., & Horner, R. H. (2008). The effects of a targeted intervention to reduce problem behaviors: Elementary school implementation of check in—check out. *Journal of Positive Behavior Interventions, 10*(1), 46–55.

Toney, H. R. (2012). The perceived self-efficacy of West Virginia public elementary school teachers to teach character education. *Theses, Dissertations and Capstones, 409.*

Trauma and Learning Policy Initiative. (n.d.). *Helping traumatized children learn.* Retrieved from https://traumasensitiveschools.org/trauma-and-learning/the-flexible-framework/

Treatment and Services Adaptation Center. (n.d.). *What is a trauma-informed school?* Retrieved from https://traumaawareschools.org/traumaInSchools

Walker, H. M., Kavanagh, K., Stiller, B., Golly, A., Severson, H. H., & Feil, E. G. (1998). First step to success: An early intervention approach for preventing school antisocial behavior. *Journal of Emotional and Behavioral Disorders, 6*(2), 66–80.

Weissberg, R. P., & Cascarino, J. (2013). Academic learning+ social-emotional learning= national priority. *Phi Delta Kappan, 95*(2), 8–13.

Wigelsworth, M., Lendrum, A., Oldfield, J., Scott, A., ten Bokkel, I., Tate, K., & Emery, C. (2016). The impact of trial stage, developer involvement and international transferability on universal social and emotional learning programme outcomes: A meta-analysis. *Cambridge Journal of Education, 46*(3), 347–376.

Winslade, J., & Monk, G. (2007). *Narrative counseling in schools: Powerful & brief,* 2nd ed. Thousand Oaks, CA: Sage.

Wlodkowski, R. J., & Ginsberg, M. B. (1995). A framework for culturally responsive teaching. *Educational Leadership, 53*(1), 17–21.

INDEX

Figures are indicated by f after the page number.

A SAGE Publishing Company

Helping educators make the greatest impact

CORWIN HAS ONE MISSION: to enhance education through intentional professional learning.

We build long-term relationships with our authors, educators, clients, and associations who partner with us to develop and continuously improve the best evidence-based practices that establish and support lifelong learning.

Solutions
YOU WANT | # Experts
YOU TRUST | # Results
YOU NEED

EVENTS

>>> **INSTITUTES**

Corwin Institutes provide large regional events where educators collaborate with peers and learn from industry experts. Prepare to be recharged and motivated!

corwin.com/institutes

ON-SITE PD

>>> **ON-SITE PROFESSIONAL LEARNING**

Corwin on-site PD is delivered through high-energy keynotes, practical workshops, and custom coaching services designed to support knowledge development and implementation.

corwin.com/pd

>>> **PROFESSIONAL DEVELOPMENT RESOURCE CENTER**

The PD Resource Center provides school and district PD facilitators with the tools and resources needed to deliver effective PD.

corwin.com/pdrc

ONLINE

>>> **ADVANCE**

Designed for K–12 teachers, Advance offers a range of online learning options that can qualify for graduate-level credit and apply toward license renewal.

corwin.com/advance

Contact a PD Advisor at (800) 831-6640 or visit www.corwin.com for more information